Hiking
Ontario's
Heartland

Hiking Ontario's Heartland

Shirley Teasdale

WHITECAP BOOKS

Vancouver / Toronto / New York

Second Printing, 1995
Revised Edition, 2000

Edited by Pat Crowe
Cover and interior design by Carolyn Deby
Cover photograph courtesy of Ontario Ministry of Culture, Tourism and Recreation
Maps and illustrations by Shayna Labelle-Beadman

Typeset by CompuType

Printed and bound in Canada

Canadian Cataloguing in Publication Data

Teasdale, Shirley.
   Hiking Ontario's heartland
   Includes index.
   ISBN 1-55285-088-9

   1. Trails—Ontario—Guidebooks. 2. Hiking—Ontario—Guidebooks. 3. Ontario—Guidebooks. I. Title.
GV199.44.C22O573 1993   917.1304'4   C93-091149-0

Please note that the hikes were accurate at the time the book was printed. However, many hikes cross private land and some landowners do withdraw permission for trails across their lands without warning. Hikers should always follow marked trails because when trails are rerouted, the trails are reblazed.

For Ken

who was with me every step of the way

and for my family

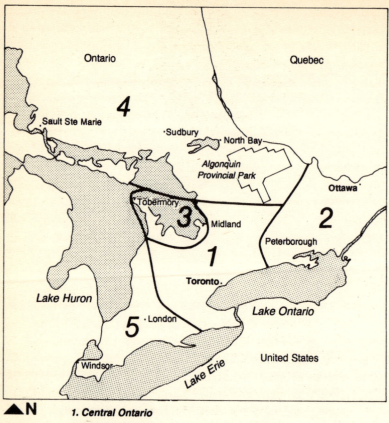

▲N

1. *Central Ontario*
2. *Eastern Ontario*
3. *Bruce-Georgian Bay*
4. *Near North*
5. *Southwestern Ontario*

CONTENTS

PREFACE

THIS BOOK includes a collection of trails designed to appeal to those looking for a few hours of interesting walking. Some may be close to home, others you may wish to try while on vacation in southern Ontario or the Near North. It does not concentrate on overnight, backpacking trails, but some sections of these longer trails are included. The hikes range from short two-to-three hour trails to those that you should allow the best part of a day to accomplish. As you walk them, slow down and take the time to savour the special places that they are, and for full enjoyment take along a couple of field guides to identify the birds, wildflowers and fungi that you see.

The book is organized into five regions of southern Ontario. Regional overviews provide hints on other trails in the region that are not detailed in the book, and telephone numbers are provided so that readers can gather information on their own.

Except for the Oak Ridges Moraine Trail in the Central Region, all trails covered in the book are clearly marked with blazes or symbols painted on trees or rocks. The Oak Ridges Moraine Trail is still in the making, and mapping and marking are under way. Established, but unmarked walking trails exist in a number of sections along the Moraine, and some sections are located in conservation areas where the trails are well blazed.

None of the trails involve trespassing, although some trails do cross private land. In all cases, however, a local hiking club, such as the Bruce Trail Association, has secured the landowner's permission for the trail to cross the property. In return, the club undertakes to the landowner that the trail will be used by walkers only, and not by cyclists or equestrians. Permission was hard won in some instances, and continuation of the privilege depends on the way we hikers conduct ourselves on the trail. Adhering to the few simple, common-sense rules in The Hiker's Code will go a long way toward keeping these privately owned paths available for public enjoyment. Bear in mind that trails over private land may sometimes be rerouted, if landowners change or withdraw the privilege. When this occurs, trail members blaze new routes, and hikers should ensure they are following these blazed routes when walking over private land.

The trails detailed here are just a sampling of the many hundreds of kilometres of trails available in this part of Ontario. It is an attempt to highlight a few that have some special feature, such as a lookout offering wonderful views, or a look at an ecosystem that is representative of a particular part of Ontario's varied landscape.

A number of the trails included here are sections of the famous Bruce Trail, which make excellent short day hikes. I have chosen to cover these in detail rather than trying to provide a brief overview of the entire 773-km trail. Many short sections are close to major populations, and the trail provides first-class walks over spectacular southern Ontario landscapes. A southern Ontario hiking book that did not include them would do its readers a disservice. The same applies to other major long-distance trails, such as the Rideau, Ganaraska and Avon. The trail associations which manage and maintain these trails publish excellent trail guidebooks. These guidebooks cover the individual trail in detail. Addresses of the major trail associations are included in the Appendix at the back of this book.

ACKNOWLEDGEMENTS

A NUMBER of people assisted in the realization of this book and I would like to thank them. I especially want to thank my husband Ken Teasdale, without whom it could not have been written; and artist-mapmaker Shayna LaBelle-Beadman for maps and such a sensitive portrayal of Ontario's wildlife and plantlife.

Thanks also to my family and friends who understood my needs; David and Denise Lott, for computer assistance and companionship on the trail; John and Sally Wright for assistance with trails on the Bruce Peninsula; Joan and Victor Huttman, for the loan of their Eastern Ontario cabin as a base for researching trails in that area; John Dadds, who lent his travelling laptop computer; Gord Teasdale for help with the Georgian Bay–Marr Lake Trail; Helen Mason for the Seguin Trail; Linda McAusland for research on Sudbury area trails.

Special thanks to Barry Westhouse of the Bruce Trail Caledon Club; Brian Wilsdon of the Elgin Trail; Rod Lafontaine of the Maitland Trail Association; Patricia Lynn of the Rideau Trail; and Geoff Dewar and Jill Leslie of Hike Ontario! These were just a few of the many who helped and provided encouragement.

Joan Bell of the Hamilton Conservation Authority was one of a number of Ontario conservation authority staff who provided advice and assistance.

Staff of the Ontario Ministry of Natural Resources were particularly helpful. They included: Don Cuddy, Bert Korporal, Gord Weedon, Leslie Joynt, Dan Boileau, Heather Bickle, John Cooper, Peter Gill, Bill Murch, Bryan Howard, Denice Wilkins and Linda Barbetti. For help with the Lake Superior trails, I'd especially like to thank staff of the Nipigon, Terrace Bay and Wawa offices of the Ministry of Natural Resources, particularly Sharon Dobush, and staff from Ontario Parks. Thanks also to Bill Dallison who hiked the trails with us.

Last, but far from least, thanks to members of the Bruce, Ganaraska, Guelph, Grand Valley, Avon and Oak Ridges Moraine trail associations. They pointed out items of particular interest, identified plants, waited patiently while I took photographs and made notes, and generally were excellent hiking companions.

INTRODUCTION

ONTARIO'S HEARTLAND can be just about anywhere in this province depending on your choice of outdoor activity. For hikers, Ontario's heartland is where the trails are, and with a few notable exceptions, the major trail systems are found in southern Ontario and the area known as Ontario's Near North. It includes those landforms known as the Precambrian Shield, the Frontenac Axis and the Niagara Peninsula, as well as farmlands, cultural and historical sites, and ecosystems ranging from spruce bogs to Carolinian Forest. All of this combines to provide hiking opportunities that can compete with the best, anywhere.

This book, then, is your invitation to explore some of the places that lie deep within the heartland of Ontario. If you have already discovered many of these secret places, it may induce memories of a happy day on the trail during those times when your hiking boots are temporarily consigned to the closet.

As well as being great exercise, hiking provides an opportunity to observe nature close to hand. Life is put into a special perspective when you stand motionless observing a red-shouldered hawk hovering over its prey, or when you marvel at the sheer, simple beauty of a trout lily in a springtime forest. It really doesn't matter how many times it happens, it's always exciting to surprise a deer close up, or watch an osprey plunging many metres to fish a trout from a lovely, lonely lake. Hiking opens up vistas we could never hope to see from a moving vehicle and reveals the innermost heart of this lovely land. You'll find places you never knew existed and learn to know them intimately.

Hiking is an exercise that can add years to your life and make those extra years more enjoyable. It is also a stress reliever and an aid to a healthy mind. For most of us who have ever spent an hour on a trail, there's a unique sense of accomplishment that comes from leaving modern transportation methods behind and travelling on foot, the way humankind has done since it rose on two legs.

It brings a special closeness to the deer, the bear, the raccoon and other creatures with whom we are privileged to share this space on our planet. Hikers feel a very special sense of responsibility to these dwellers of forest and field and to the home we share. Many hiking club members spend time maintaining trails so that other hikers can stay on paths in sensitive areas and therefore avoid degrading environmentally sensitive plants or habitat. They leave behind no signs that they have been there, and pick up the detritus left behind by the less thoughtful.

Many of the trails covered in this book would not exist were it not for these hiking club volunteers. They give their time, energy and money maintaining the trails and lobbying for their continued existence. We owe them dearly. If you are not already a hiking club member, consider joining a club and supporting its work. Club members are warm, friendly people who will welcome you to the association and to their group hikes. Since you should never hike alone, joining a group hike is a perfect way for singles, or people from one-hiker families to get out on the trail.

If you cannot join a club, but use trails supported by a volunteer organization, you may wish to consider making a donation to their work now and again. This will help to ensure that the trails in Ontario's heartland will remain to be discovered and enjoyed by the generations of hikers who will follow after us.

TRAIL RATINGS

The following provides a rough guide to the Degree of Difficulty ratings given to individual trails.

Easy

Trails given this rating are usually short, over flat terrain with few hills or challenges. No special boots or equipment are needed. The trails are generally suitable for young children and the average senior who does not walk often. They are also good shape-up walks for the out-of-practice.

Moderate

Most trails fit into this category. Moderate trails offer a bit more of a workout than the easy trails; they may be longer in length and involve some hill climbing. Comfortable shoes or boots are recommended. While not always necessary, a small backpack that can carry lunch and drinks adds to the enjoyment of the walk. Suitable for older children and the average adult.

Moderate to Challenging

A little more challenging than a moderate trail, due to the length or level of climbing involved. The trail may include walking along cliff edges where caution must be exercised. Hiking boots are recommended, as well as a small backpack to carry drinks and lunch. Suitable for most active adults.

Challenging

This may include a long trail in a remote area where help may be difficult to obtain quickly in an emergency. Hikers should always carry food and water, map and compass, and emergency supplies such as a small first-aid kit. The trail may involve some rock climbing, and should usually be done in optimum weather conditions. Hiking boots are recommended. Suitable for the experienced hiker.

Central Ontario

REGIONAL OVERVIEW

CENTRAL ONTARIO spreads like a fan from its base on Lake Ontario. It is the most populated of all regions of Ontario and its green spaces and recreational areas are heavily used and jealously guarded. It includes such prominent landforms as part of the Niagara Escarpment and all of the Oak Ridges Moraine. These provide first-class hiking opportunities. Other hiking opportunities are found in river valleys, farmlands and Lake Ontario marshes.

The world-renowned **Bruce Trail** starts in Niagara and passes through much of Central Ontario on its way to Bruce–Georgian Bay. To explore sections of the trail that are not outlined in this book, you should acquire the latest edition of the *Guide to the Bruce Trail* (see Appendix).

In the eastern part of the region, the **Ganaraska Trail** starts at the shore of Lake Ontario. It winds north through farmlands to a wilderness region of tundra-like proportions until it intersects with the Bruce Trail near Georgian Bay. A detailed guidebook is available from the association (see Appendix).

Another major trail system is the **Grand Valley Trail**, which starts in the hills south of Orangeville and follows the Grand River to Lake Erie. The **Guelph Radial Trail** and the **Speed River Trail**, both maintained by the Guelph Trail Club, offer hiking opportunities in the attractive countryside around the City of Guelph. The **Merritt Trail** follows the route of the three Welland Canals between Port Dalhousie on Lake Ontario and Port Colborne on

Lake Erie. Trail details are available from The Welland Canal Preservation Association, 52 Lakeport Road, P.O. Box 1224, St. Catharines, Ontario L2R 7A7, or from Hike Ontario!

There are also a number of publicly owned regional forests that provide trails. North of Toronto is the **York Regional Forest** which is spread out into a number of widely separated tracts but which offers enormous potential for hikers. A number of these tracts are located between Woodbine Avenue and Highway 48, just north of the Bloomington Sideroad, near Aurora. For more information and directions, contact the Ministry of Natural Resources, Maple District Office, (416) 832-2761.

One of the best-kept secrets from a hiking point of view is the number of abandoned rail lines that are being developed into all-purpose trails. Since 1970 almost 3,000 km of rail lines in Ontario have been abandoned, and most of these lie in southern Ontario. The tracks have been ripped up and, in many cases, bridges have been removed. Recreationists see these abandoned lines as perfect trail potential and groups are raising funds to buy them and replace bridges; a not inexpensive proposition. To date, some 21 trails with a total length of 313 km have been developed in the province.

The **Sutton Trail** is an abandoned line managed by the Ministry of Natural Resources in conjunction with the York Regional Forest. It runs north from Zephyr Station to Sutton on Lake Simcoe, a distance of about 12 km, paralleling Highway 48. In Sutton, access the trail from the first turning on the right south of the Sutton District High School. From the south, access it from Holborn Road, east of Highway 48 at Zephyr Station.

One of the better-known rail trails is the **Uthoff Trail**, 12 km north of Orillia. After initial opposition from local landowners (who now support the trail) an 8-km stretch was opened in 1991. It is now being extended to an 11-km linear trail and is operated as a nature walk by the Orillia Naturalists Club. It runs north to south and is accessed from its southern end at Division Road and the 6th Concession. At its northern end it is accessed from Wilson's Point Road. Hike Ontario! can supply more details.

The Grand River Conservation Authority has acquired rights to an 18-km stretch of abandoned rail line running from **Cambridge to Paris**. The Section from Galt to Paris travels through beautiful Carolinian forest alongside the Grand River, and it is accessed from just south of town. Obtain more information from the Grand River Conservation Authority at (519) 621-2761. The Grand has plans for more abandoned rail line acquisitions as funding permits.

An 18-km stretch of the old Toronto, Hamilton and Buffalo Railway has been acquired by the Hamilton and Region Conservation Authority. This runs from Highway 2 in Hamilton to Field Road in Jerseyville. This major acquisition will allow a number of new loops with the **Dundas Valley Trail System** and the Bruce Trail. More information is available from the Hamilton and Region Conservation Authority at (416) 525-2181.

Many conservation areas in the Central Region are on lands on the Niagara Escarpment or the Oak Ridges Moraine. This means they offer some of the best hiking opportunities in the province.

North of Toronto on Airport Road, just south of Mono Mills, is **Glen Haffy Conservation Area**. Trails lead to magnificent views from the Niagara Escarpment and through lovely hardwood forest. The Bruce Trail runs through it. Just southeast is the **Albion Hills Conservation Area**, located north of Bolton on Highway 50. This conservation area is on the Oak Ridges Moraine and there are streams, forests and rolling hills to hike on. Call the Metro Toronto and Region Conservation Authority at (416) 661-6600 for more details.

West of Toronto is **Terra Cotta**, near Georgetown. Hiking here is on the Niagara Escarpment and through the woods. Follow Winston Churchill Boulevard, northwest of Norval, about 10 km to the village of Terra Cotta, then watch for signs to the conservation area. **Rockwood Conservation Area**, east of Guelph, offers trails around a pretty lake. Access is from south of Highway 7 at Rockwood. Other fine trails are at **Hilton Falls**, and **Crawford Lake** both in the Milton area and on the Niagara Escarpment. Call the Halton Region Conservation Authority at (416) 336-1158 for information on these two.

The Royal Botanical Gardens in Hamilton is well known for walks, as well as being the home of the Bruce Trail office. Trails are around Cootes Paradise marsh, and maps are available. More information is available from (416) 527-1158.

There are many lovely conservation areas in the Niagara region, which offer hiking opportunities, particularly **Ball's Falls**. Contact the Niagara Region Conservation Authority at (416) 227-1013.

East of Toronto, check out the **Ken Reid Conservation Area** north of Lindsay. Owned by the Kawartha Region Conservation Authority, it occupies a spit of land on the south end of Sturgeon Lake. The trails explore marshland and forest, and an abandoned rail line in the area adds potential for loops. You should know, however, that the abandoned rail line has an approximate 31-m gap in the trail in the middle of the marsh. For more information call (705) 887-3112.

Some provincial parks offer hiking opportunities. One of the best bets is **Bronte Creek** near Burlington, which has an intricate network of trails in the deep and lovely creek valley. It is accessed from the Queen Elizabeth Highway at Exit 109, Burloak Drive.

North of Toronto there are trails in **Springwater Provincial Park** near Barrie, and **Earl Rowe Provincial Park** near Alliston. More information on provincial parks can be obtained from the Ministry of Natural Resources at the address listed in the Appendix.

Hiking Ontario's Heartland

Grand Valley Trail

East Garafraxa Town Line to Belwood Lake

• **LENGTH:** 15 km (5 hours) • **DEGREE OF DIFFICULTY:** Moderate
• **TYPE OF TRAIL:** Linear • **LOCATION:** Belwood

HOW TO GET THERE:

Belwood is on Wellington Road 26, northeast of Fergus, between Highways 6 and 25. This trail requires car jockeying. There is a small parking area on the south side of the Belwood Lake bridge where the trail ends. Park a second car at the start of the trail by driving south on Wellington Road 26, turning left onto Wellington Road 18 and driving about 5 km to the 12th Sideroad (church

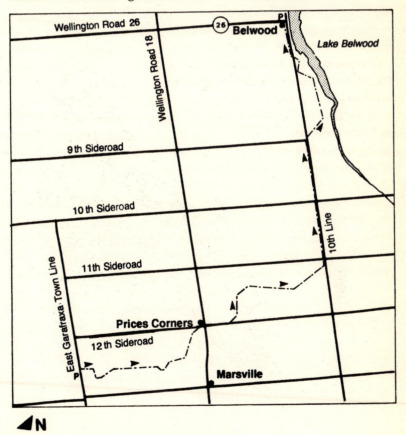

and graveyard will be on the southeast corner). Drive south on the 12th Sideroad to the East Garafraxa Town Line. Turn left and drive about 500 m until you see the white triangle of the Grand Valley Trail Association on the north side of the road. You may park on the shoulder of the road.

• • •

The Grand Valley trail generally traces the valley of the Grand River as it winds some 250 km through Ontario farmland and the rapidly growing cities of Cambridge, Kitchener, Waterloo, Paris, and Brantford to Lake Erie. It is a trail that is best done in late summer or fall, when there is less chance of seasonal flooding, the mosquitos have gone, and the fruits of a bountiful land hang heavy on tree and bush. The trail crosses mostly private lands so by walking the fields later in the growing season hikers avoid trampling a farmer's tender young plants. Periods of rain can leave puddles at the edges of ploughed fields so boots are a good idea.

While the stretch in the area of Lake Belwood does not have the rugged appeal or vistas offered by such trails as the Bruce, it is very much a trail for those who like a ramble in the country. It skirts the edges of fields where wild apples hang like gaudy festive baubles. At times it winds through damp woodlots where rare orchids glimmer with pristine whiteness. It goes on through fields high with spiky grass and past corn that seems to have grown higher than the elephant's eye celebrated in song. Along the way, it follows quiet country roads and enters sweet-smelling cedar forests as it winds towards Lake Belwood, which was formed by the damming of the Grand River. It is Ontario farming country at its finest.

Although paths are not well-defined through fields and woods, and traversing numerous planted fields can be confusing, the trail is so well marked with white blazes, thanks to the dedication of trail volunteers, there is little danger of losing your way.

From the East Garafraxa Town Line, the trail runs along the edge of a cornfield in a northwesterly direction. The countryside is open with long views of rolling hills to the west. At the top of the field a double white blaze signifies a turn to the right and the path runs alongside a young plantation of Scots pines. On past this, the trail passes by a treed area, thick with raspberry bushes and elderberries, towards a farm. Canada geese honk and take flight as the path turns left onto a farm laneway and skirts a small wetland fringed with cattails. The burnished colours of fall are found in the purple New England aster, goldenrod, and mullein, and in the sugar maple bush beyond the wetland.

The trail continues to the end of the laneway and turns right into a field, following hedgerow and fence line. A mountain ash literally drips with brilliant scarlet berries. The path traces the edge of a series of fields where a variety of crops is in various stages of harvest. It is very muddy and marshy in places. In a few minutes the path skirts a pond with an apple tree on its banks. In the pond are the easily identifiable leaves of the broad-leaved arrowhead.

The path crosses a culvert and heads for a small bush, emerging close to a stile. A large flock of mallards rises like a cloud of locusts from a small pond in the field, darkening the sky. Cross the stile and walk roughly southwest to the hedgerow, then turn right until you come to another stile. Over the stile the path turns right, passing to the left of a barn and then to the right of a lovely little pond until it comes to a graveyard on the 12th Sideroad. Turn right and follow the road about 300 m until you see a blaze on your left next to a sign reading "Golden Hylite," just before reaching the hydro pylons.

Walk on the grass to the right of the private driveway and follow the path as it veers to the right. The hedgerow is thick with raspberry bushes, chokecherry, elderberry, and mixed fall flowers.

Central Ontario

The pathway gives way to fields and there are views of gently rolling open country before the trail enters a young bush where, glowing like jewels on the forest floor, is a bed of ladies tresses orchids.

The path wends its inevitable way through fields, beside swamps formed by beaver dams, and in and out of woodlots until it reaches a little glade, ringed by cedars and threaded through by a clear stream. A perfect spot for lunch. The stream even yields stalks of watercress to spice up sandwiches. This is about the half-way point in the hike.

After following the stream a short way the trail climbs up a steep little bank beside a cement culvert to the 10th Line. Turn left and follow this about 3 km until you pass the 9th Sideroad. It is easy walking here, on the gravel road between country estate properties. Keep an eye out for the odd vehicle. Just before you come to a bridge with an orange and black traffic sign, turn into a cedar bush on your right.

The floor of this cedar bush is awash with tiny bulblet ferns. From here, the trail enters a pine plantation tracing the line of a cedar rail fence until it reaches the high banks of the Grand River. The river is astonishingly wide here, considering it still has some 200 km to travel before reaching Lake Erie.

The walking now becomes very pleasant as the trail winds for about 1 km along the river bank and through a mature cedar bush. Mossy stones litter the forest floor and an interesting collection of fungi can be seen. A wide stream may be crossed by stepping stones, or across a living cedar bridge.

The trail emerges once again onto the 10th Line, turns right for about 50 m, then enters into the bush again. It veers towards the river, which is now widening into Lake Belwood, then tacks back towards the 10th Line and follows it about 1 km to the parking area at the bridge.

Caledon Hills

Abandoned Rail Line

- **LENGTH:** 10 km (3 hours) • **DEGREE OF DIFFICULTY:** Easy
- **TYPE OF TRAIL:** Linear • **LOCATION:** Caledon East

HOW TO GET THERE:

This trail runs between the villages of Inglewood, west of High-way 10, and Caledon East on Airport Road. Because it is linear it will require car jockeying. In Inglewood there is parking at the Arena. There is also parking for about six vehicles on the shoulder

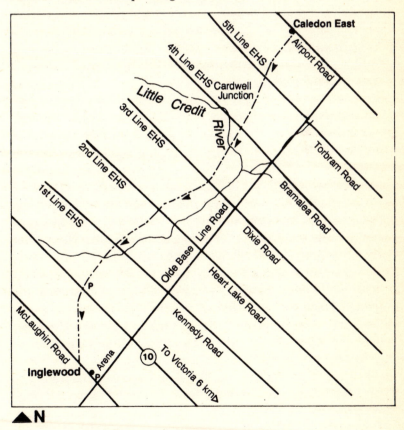

of Highway 10 near the Ken Whillans Resource Management Area, about 6 km north of Victoria (a 2-km walk along the trail from Inglewood). Arrange a drop-off, or second parking on Airport Road, just south of Caledon East at the bottom of the hill. Look for a path leading off to the west.

• • •

This is an easy trail that is ideal for the novice hiker, or for anyone looking for a pleasant country walk. Because it once carried the steel tracks of a railroad, there are no hills. This means it is a no-sweat hike on a summer day, or, if you live not far away, a perfect summer evening walk. The autumn colours of the Caledon Hills are unsurpassed anywhere so it is a particularly good fall walk. In spring, the section between Highway 10 and the 1st Line is prime mosquito country due to the large wetlands associated with the Little Credit River that lie on both sides of the trail.

The trail involves crossing the extremely busy Highway 10. If this does not appeal, you can shorten the walk by 2 km by eliminating the stretch between Highway 10 and Inglewood. The trail crosses five quiet sideroads between Airport Road and Highway 10. If car jockeying is a problem, you can still do part of this walk by contriving a loop, using these sideroads and a parallel sideroad such as Olde Base Line to the south, or 5 Sideroad to the north. For example, you could park near the trail entrance on the 5th Line EHS (Torbram Road), walk the trail, then turn right onto the 4th Line EHS (Bramalea Road), turn right again onto 5 Sideroad and finally right again onto the 5th Line EHS. This would total about 8 km.

The trail follows the route of an old Canadian National line between Hamilton and Barrie which was abandoned as a transportation route in 1967. Built in the 1870s as the Hamilton and Northwestern Railway, it became part of the Grand Trunk Railway System in 1888 before being taken over by CN. It is now owned by the Town of Caledon for use as a recreational trail. The route also forms a section of the Bruce Trail and, although signs prohibit its use by motorized vehicles, there is occasional use by off-road vehicles. You may also find yourself sharing the trail with equestrians.

On leaving and entering the trail at some of the sideroads you will notice No Trespassing signs. These do not refer to use of the trail but are a caution not to leave the trail to explore the surrounding countryside, which is privately owned.

The path is softly packed sand and gravel, which is akin to walking in snow as it does not provide a firm base. In places you will notice that narrow paths have been made to run parallel with the track, especially where there is an embankment. You may wish to follow these narrow paths at times because they reveal views of rolling hills that are sometimes hidden by the regular track lying in the hollow of the embankment.

Be warned, though. Poison ivy is rampant in places along this trail, and it is most frequent on the stretch between Highway 10 and the 1st Line EHS.

Views of Devil's Pulpit on the Niagara Escarpment are visible from many places on the trail. This is the line of hills dead ahead as you walk from Caledon East.

Leaving Caledon East you will walk through a mostly forested area, crossing the Centreville Creek before reaching the 5th Line. Wildflowers are abundant, and open spaces at the edge of the track are brilliant with wild bergamot, phlox, creeping bellflower, black-eyed Susans and coreopsis, as well as the usual Queen Anne's lace, evening primrose and tall, stately mulleins.

Half-way between the 5th and 4th Lines you will come to what remains of Cardwell Junction. Today, only two huge stone abutments stand at either side of the track, but in its heyday, the Toronto, Grey and Bruce Railway line (eventually the Canadian Pacific Railway) crossed the CN line at this point by means of a high stone bridge. (The TG&B line no longer exists but at the turn of the century was famous for its Great Horseshoe Curve, constructed a few kilometres northwest of Cardwell Junction, where the railroad negotiated the Niagara Escarpment. The curve was the scene of a spectacular crash in 1907, when a train carrying vacationers to the Toronto International Exhibition jumped the tracks killing seven and injuring more than 100 people.)

The trail continues through a variety of terrain, much like an English country lane. Sometimes it passes through open country where the rolling, forested Caledon Hills may be seen to the near north, and sometimes through wetlands where pink Joe pye-weed and blue vervain threatens to be overtaken by the ever-menacing march of the lovely but deadly purple loosestrife.

At times the trail is closed in by cedar bush and at other times it passes pine plantations. Sometimes it travels between high embankments and sometimes it is built high with the banks falling away at either side. Deer tracks are numerous. Catbirds, cardinals and American goldfinch are a few of the birds that call from the nearby woods. Apple trees, not content to provide their bounty, are also home to grape vines that hang heavy with fruit. Just past the 2nd Line, the path is a veritable sweet pea alley where it is lined with this lovely wildflower that has escaped from cultivated gardens.

The stretch between the 1st Line and Highway 10 crosses and recrosses the Little Credit, a lovely stream where pristine white turtlehead and beds of jewelweed grow beyond banks awash with poison ivy. (It is said that rubbing the stems of jewelweed on limbs that have been exposed to poison ivy is a good antidote to effects of the noxious plant.) Large wetlands stretch on both sides of the path, heavily overgrown with cattails. A belted kingfisher surveys his domain from the high spire of a dead tree. Solid old timbers that once supported railroad tracks now serve as footbridges over the stream. Here and there small gnawed tree trunks are signs of recent beaver activity in the stream, and some broken turtle eggs attest to predation by skunks or raccoons.

Across Highway 10, the trail enters the Ken Whillans Resource Management Area. This area of public land was named for the late Ken Whillans, a long-time Brampton councillor and mayor of Brampton until he met with accidental death while on vacation in 1990.

The trail winds through this forested area until it emerges on the main street in the village of Inglewood.

Copeland Forest Trails

- **LENGTH:** 2 to 13 km (1 to 4 hours) • **DEGREE OF DIFFICULTY:** Easy
- **TYPE OF TRAIL:** Loop • **LOCATION:** Orillia/Mount St. Louis

HOW TO GET THERE:

You can reach the Copeland Forest from Highway 400, north of Barrie (west of Orillia) by taking Exit 121 and turning east onto Highway 93. Almost immediately turn north onto Ingram Road, which runs parallel to Highway 400. Drive about 6.5 km to the main parking area.

• • •

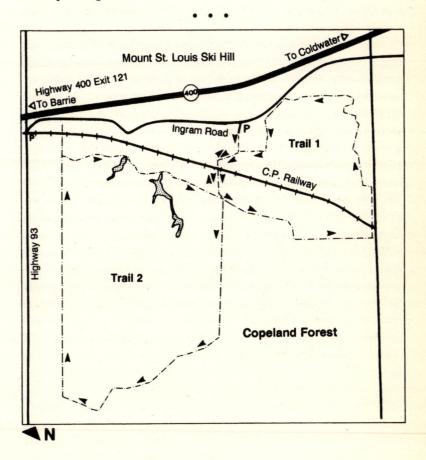

The Copeland Forest is one of the loveliest forests in southern Ontario. It is super in spring, fabulous in the fall. The forest is full of lush undergrowth, towering old pines, unusual wildflowers and ferns, and, of course, hectares of maples, oaks, beeches, birches and evergreens. If you are lucky, you may also catch a glimpse of the rare wild turkey. The trails are ideal for the beginning hiker, or one who hasn't been on the trail for a while and needs to limber up and get the old hiking legs in shape. It is also part of the 200-km Ganaraska Trail that winds from Port Hope on Lake Ontario to Glen Huron, near Georgian Bay.

Sold in 1978 to the province by the Copeland Brothers, a family logging operation, the forest is an example of how effective regeneration can be achieved. A very few hectares show obvious signs of tree farming—planting of single species for future crops. This is a section of tall pines, planted like soldiers in rows perhaps 40 years ago. The thick canopy allows no undergrowth on the forest floor to soften the angles, nor are there hardwoods mixed in to provide variety. But this is a very small piece of the entire forest and the rest of it is beautiful.

The forest offers a variety of trails so you can tailor a loop to your particular demand on any particular day. We chose to start from a parking lot on the northeast end of the forest, but the same effect can be achieved from using a parking lot at the northwest end, accessible from Ingram Road. Our trail led out of the parking lot to the south, then in an easterly direction, looping around until it brought us back to the parking lot, a walk of about 1 hour.

A second foray followed the first trail for about 500 m and continued due south deep into the forest, where there is a group camping area and a source of drinking water. Here, after a lunch stop, we wound westwards, eventually turning onto a trail that ran straight as an arrow towards the north end of the forest. Turning eastwards we passed a couple of lovely ponds, eventually returning to the parking lot. The entire trip covered some 13 km and took about 4 hours, including a half-hour lunch stop.

From the parking lot the trail heads south over wide paths well-carpeted with pine needles and last year's leaves, for an ideal walking surface. The woods smell rich with decay and in spring, trilliums huge and white, pink and painted, wave bravely on the forest floor, and fringed polygalas peep from behind the trees. In about 500 m the trail opens into a leafy glade with picnic tables. Turning onto a left fork, the trail continues over a railroad track where there are huge white spruce that are some of the oldest and biggest in Ontario. They are not hard to spot.

In another 500 m or so the trail turns left into yet another grassy clearing and eventually leads to a gate giving onto the 3rd Concession. Turn left and walk the road a little way, recrossing the tracks before turning back into the bush next to a No Hunting sign and a fence labelled "17."

The trail is a little overgrown here so look carefully for signs of the path that will lead you uphill. Before going, however, investigate the swamp at the bottom. At the right time of year you will find Solomon's seal, jack-in-the-pulpit, and a number of unusual ferns.

The trail winds through the bush here but eventually leads back to the parking lot. Cross the parking lot and again take the path that leads due south. Cross the railroad tracks again and follow the path through a variety of forest ecosystems from mixed hardwoods to hardwoods and evergreens. Watch in the open spaces for the scarlet tanager and large crested flycatcher.

Central Ontario

The trail veers to the west passing the group camping area until it reaches a clearing where there is an untreated water source. Look for signs of deer around this area. This is a good lunch break spot.

From here the trail meanders westwards until it makes a sharp right turn onto a straight path. You will know you are heading north because you will have a great view of Mount St. Louis dead ahead. This ridge was the site of a Huron village when Champlain was exploring the area in the early 1600s. Archaeological evidence shows that the Copeland Forest was an important source of food even for the early aboriginals. Spear points dating from the Archaic Period (5,000 B.C. to 500 B.C.) have been found in the forest.

The trail nears the northern perimeter of the forest and turns eastwards once again close to the site of old pioneer farmsteads. Today a huge shed occupies the site. Pioneers tried farming here but the sandy soils proved to be poor for crops. Most supplemented their incomes with logging. Eventually, in the mid-1800s, commercial loggers moved in, stripping the forest without much regard for its longterm health. At one time, the timber from this area serviced some 25 mills that operated in Medonte and Matchedash Townships. Ownership and timber rights to the area went through numerous hands and the mills floundered until Charles Ernest Copeland bought two mills and 1,320 hectares of the forest in 1922.

Charles and his sons revitalized the mills, bringing some prosperity to the area and eventually acquiring more property. More importantly, in 1930 they started a massive reforestation program, planting 800,000 seedlings.

The results of that farsighted replanting program are evident today and hikers are major beneficiaries being able to enjoy this beautiful forest.

Forks of the Credit

- **LENGTH:** 6 km (2 hours) • **DEGREE OF DIFFICULTY:** Easy
- **TYPE OF TRAIL:** Loop • **LOCATION:** Caledon

HOW TO GET THERE:

Take Highway 10 to Caledon, then drive west on Highway 24. Turn south on 2nd Line WHS and travel past a gravel pit. Look for the Forks of the Credit Provincial Park sign to your right at the start of a laneway. The parking lot is at the end of the laneway.

• • •

This trail loops through the Forks of the Credit Provincial Park. It is notable because it is here that the cliffs and cuestas of the

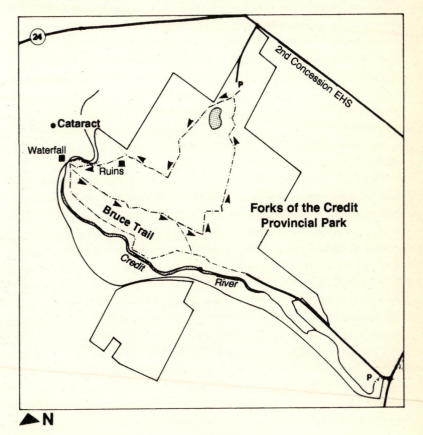

rugged Niagara Escarpment meet the rolling hills of the Oak Ridges Moraine.

The trail includes a visit to the Credit Falls, where the Credit River plunges over a rocky ledge near the village of Cataract. Long known to local aboriginal people, the first white man to see the falls was William Grant. In 1818, Grant was "searching in this roadless, broken, forested country for the mythical gold of Caledon Mountain," according to a local history, *The Perkins Bull Collection: Towns and Villages of Peel County*.

In the early 1800s, men died in the snows between here and the town of York looking for gold. No gold was found but miners did find salt, which was exploited for some years. The area really became industrialized when a fine sandstone was discovered and quarried. A railroad was built when it was realized that building stone for the growing town of York (now Toronto) could be quarried and shipped more cheaply from here than from Ohio. Consequently, sandstone from this area was used to build the Ontario Legislative Building in Toronto.

The area's other claim to fame was—and still is—springs of clear water that flow on the hillsides. In the early 1900s, the Forks of the Credit bottling works of Mr. J.J. McLaughlin invented a new drink, using this source. Today it is known as Canada Dry Ginger Ale.

None of this is evident now. Today, this is rural Ontario at its finest, with tiny villages dotting the valleys and estate homes rubbing shoulders with log cabins that once were summer cottages.

Trails in the Forks of the Credit Provincial Park are over hills, old farm fields, through hardwood and cedar forests, and along the top of steep bluffs.

The waterfalls and ruins of an old, but historically important mill are reached at the half-way point of the trail. The other attraction of this walk is that it may be varied and considerably lengthened by numerous side trips.

From the parking lot the trail branches off into paths "A" and "B" which are the beginning and end of the loop. Follow the "B" trail which branches off to the right of the main path.

This leads downhill, past a small kidney-shaped kettle lake on the left. The lake lies in a deep bowl, with its most easily accessible shoreline close to the trail. Look here for signs of beaver. There is a path around the north side. If you take this you will have to return on the same path, or climb upwards through waist-high prairie grassland to regain the trail farther on.

On the right of the path where it passes the lake is a small pond which is a popular spot for birds. Past the lake, the path climbs steeply to the top of rolling meadows. In spring and summer the meadows are sweet with a variety of wildflowers. This is open grassland, but scattered clumps of old trees provide shade for a picnic.

Following the line of the hill, the trail dips into a valley and skirts the dried-up hollow of an ancient kettle lake before climbing again and heading northwest. At the top, some of the best views of the entire trip may be seen. To the south rears Devil's Pulpit and the tree-topped cliffs and exposed rockfaces of the Niagara Escarpment. To the east, the rolling hills of the Oak Ridges Moraine stretch to the horizon.

The path descends again and at the T-junction there is a choice of cutting the trip short by turning left and making for the junction with Trail "A," or turning right and continuing on to the waterfall viewing platform.

The path now follows an old tree-lined farm road until it reaches the next junction where there is a sign giving directions to the waterfall. The path turns left.

There is a detour here if you want to leave the main route and get close to the river. Simply follow the farm road on past the junction and down the hill. At the bottom of the hill a narrow path goes off to the left, along the banks of the Credit. This is a very pretty area but the path is overgrown. If you take this route you should return by the same path because the river banks are thickly forested with cedar and are steep and difficult, if not impossible, to negotiate.

Continuing on to the waterfall, turn left and you will see an old farmstead. If you poke around you will see where steps led to the front door. Some lilacs and a clump of peonies show where the farmhouse garden was planted. Close by you can easily see the remains of the barn foundation and a surprisingly sturdy-looking silo almost overtaken by a stand of sumac. An 1877 map shows this land was probably owned by J.F. Scott, an early settler.

The trail now edges towards some large cedars on the edge of the Credit's gorge. Sturdy new steps and landings lead down the cliff face to the waterfall viewing platform. A series of self-interpretive displays and the ruins of an old mill tell the story of the river and of the pioneers who harnessed its energy.

You can make another choice of route here. After viewing the falls, you can return up the steps and continue along the top of the gorge, or you can follow the path as it drops gently down the cliff face and through the woods towards the banks of the Credit. This is a nice walk if you want to be close to the river but can be muddy and slippery in damp weather. An intersecting path about 1 km farther on leads up a steep bank to the top of the cliff to rejoin the "A" trail.

Back at the top of the viewing platform steps, the path joins a Bruce Trail side trail for part of the return trip and becomes the "A" Trail. Here it skirts the edge of the Credit River gorge, and at times you will find you are walking level with the tops of the trees that line the slopes of the gorge. The view in places here is magnificent, but because most of this area is forested you occasionally will need to leave the path and walk to the cliff edge to see it. About 500 m along, the Bruce side trail meanders into the forest along a narrow track on the extreme edge of the bluffs. If it has been raining, or there are wet leaves around, you will need to exercise caution because the path can be slippery.

FARMSTEAD RUINS

Trail "A," meanwhile, continues along a wide path. Where it turns eastward to return to the parking lot, you have an option of continuing southward and following an unmarked trail through an old orchard and alongside a young pine forest before cutting across the fields and back to the parking lot.

The main trail turns away from the cliff edge and heads towards the ruins of an old stone farmhouse, then turns right onto a cart track. To your left you can see the kettle lake in its deep hollow. Small turtles like to sun themselves on old logs at this end of the lake. Keep an eye on the pine plantation to your far right for occasional glimpses of white-tailed deer before returning to the parking lot.

Dufferin Quarry Bridge Trail

Bruce Trail

• **LENGTH:** 12 km (4 hours) • **DEGREE OF DIFFICULTY:** Moderate
• **TYPE OF TRAIL:** Loop • **LOCATION:** Milton

HOW TO GET THERE:

Take Highway 401 to Milton, exiting onto Highway 25 North, and driving approximately 1 km to the 5th Sideroad. Turn left and follow 5th Sideroad to 6th Line. Turn right and drive north 6.1 km, passing Sheridan College Heavy Equipment School on the east side, to a small parking lot on the west side. The trail starts across the road.

• • •

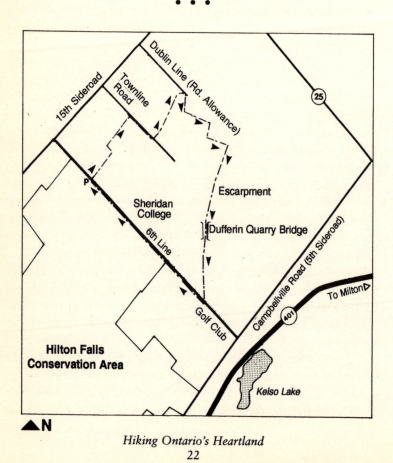

This is a fabulous trail with its only flaw being a 3 km stretch on a paved highway, but there are few hikes in Ontario that offer more dramatic features. It is part of the Hilton Falls Side Trail of the Bruce Trail. This section of the trail once followed another path for much of the way, but it has been rerouted because of an active quarrying operation. Hikers should always ensure that the trail has not been rerouted again, because parts of it do cross private land and sometimes the routes change to accommodate land-owners' wishes. Always follow the trail markers to ensure you are on the trail.

After a fairly long walk through the woods from the start of the trail, the path follows the edge of the Niagara Escarpment for per-haps 1 km, offering splendid views over the flat plains that sur-round the Toronto area. The cliffs are also home to the famous 900-year-old cedars that were discovered and identified only a few years ago. You'll find yourself striding over deep fissures that drop to a black nothingness and walking over narrow plateaus centi-metres from the unfenced edge of the escarpment. If children accom-pany you on this hike you will need to supervise them carefully.

You will also cross the impressive Dufferin Quarry Bridge. The building of this structure was spearheaded by the Bruce Trail Association and it is limited to foot traffic. It bridges a gap in the huge cliff face caused by quarrying and forges another link in the famous Bruce Trail chain.

The trail starts from a small parking lot on the 6th Line. Cross the road to the east side and walk across a wooden bridge over a swampy area. It is marked by blue blazes. The trail heads east-wards through the forest, where the undergrowth is lush with wild rhubarb, rose mallow, may-apple and several varieties of ferns.

The trail is in good shape and flat for the most part with a small ridge to be climbed. It travels through the forest at the south end of a working gravel pit, jogging slightly to the north at one point, then continuing eastwards about 2 km until it meets Town Line Road.

Turn right onto Town Line and walk south 500 m, following the blue blazes, then look for the Hilton Falls Side Trail marker show-ing where the trail leaves the sideroad on the east side. There is a farm immediately to the south of the entrance. The trail follows a wide path here over old fields. In the field to the north, a whitetail deer gazes at us for some time before bounding into the bush.

Follow the blue signs for about 500 m, before coming to a short stretch of gravel path that veers off to the right, following the Dublin Line Road allowance (there are no markings to show this). On the left are the remains of an old reservoir, and the path you are following appears to travel over what used to be a residential community or homesite.

Follow the path over the old field and into the woods, but look carefully for the blue blazes marking the entrance. The trail here is a bit confusing because the trail forks, while the road allowance continues. Take the trail to the right, marked Hilton Falls Side Trail, which follows a narrow path through the woods. (If you miss this and continue along the road allowance, you will meet up with the trail again.) The trail meanders through the woods, with a small pond to your right, and eventually meets and crosses the road allowance. Look carefully for the blue trail blazes. The trail now starts to wind upwards through very rocky terrain. The footing is quite treacherous, especially in the fall when a blanket of leaves covers the rocks.

After about 500 m, look carefully for a turn to the left and follow the path as it comes down off a small ridge. You will see a wetland at the bottom. The path winds downward to the other side of the swamp, then starts to climb again.

This is typical Niagara Escarpment country, with its scattered and abundant moss-covered and fossil-imprinted limestone rocks, from which sprout dainty ferns.

This new path is extremely rocky, climbs slightly, and leads to the very edge of the Niagara Escarpment. At first, trees lining the edge obscure the view, except for glimpses between the branches. When the views open up they are dramatic, revealing the surrounding plains far below.

The path winds dangerously close to the edge, with a sheer drop of some 20 m. There is a golf course immediately below and the view stretches eastwards to take in the highrises of Mississauga. You will stride over a number of deep fissures. One that is especially deep appears to be the edge of a freestanding cliff. **Exercise caution!**

Following the line of the escarpment, the path heads first south, and then west offering excellent views of Rattlesnake Point. This is the prominent scarp face that towers over the town of Milton.

The path veers away from the cliff face for a little way and soon arrives at the Dufferin Quarry Bridge. The bridge is as much a remarkable feat of engineering as it is a testimony to the persistence of a group of volunteers. Members of the Bruce Trail Association co-ordinated a fundraising project to build the bridge. Money came from the Ontario government and corporate sponsors, as well as the quarry operators and Bruce Trail members. The bridge spans a gap between two cliffs high above the roadway that leads into the massive Dufferin Aggregates quarry.

By now, you will have been on the trail some 2.5 hours. From the bridge, the trail turns left towards the escarpment edge again, following white blazes. The path is very rocky but bordered by much greenery in places and wildflowers such as jewelweed. It continues along the line of the cliff, climbing up and down a series of ridges. Here the ancient cedars cling to the cliff top and face. You will see some remarkably tortured trunks and limbs. Please leave them undisturbed, as befits their great age. Watch out for large patches of poison ivy bordering the path.

You will follow this path for about 1 km, encountering some long crevices and cave-like chasms before squeezing through a rock crevice and emerging onto the 6th Line once again opposite the golf course. Turn right and walk north, keeping to the west side of this busy road. The parking lot is about a 3 km walk from here. An alternative route, though much longer, is to cross 6th Line and go into the Hilton Falls Conservation Area, then follow the Hilton Falls Side Trail back to the parking lot.

Dundas Valley Headwaters Trail

Dundas Valley Conservation Area

- **LENGTH:** 14 km (4.5 hours) • **DEGREE OF DIFFICULTY:** Moderate
- **TYPE OF TRAIL:** Loop • **LOCATION:** Dundas

HOW TO GET THERE:

Follow Highway 403 to where it joins Highway 2, then go west on Highway 2 approximately 3 km to Highway 52. Drive north on Highway 52 to Governors Road (Highway 399). Turn east onto Governors Road and drive until you see the sign indicating the entrance to the Dundas Valley Conservation Area on the south side.

• • •

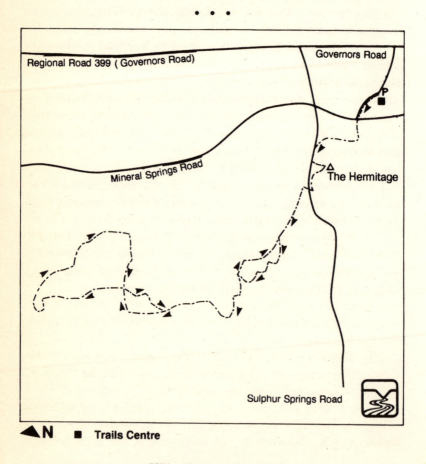

▲N   ■ Trails Centre

There are not enough superlatives to describe the Dundas Valley. It is, quite simply, magnificent. The views start the minute you enter the park gates and they don't stop until you leave. This conservation area, which occupies about 1,200 ha of Niagara Escarpment country on the western fringe of Hamilton, caters to the hiker by offering some 50 km of trails. The trails wander through stretches of lovely Carolinian forest. They meander through deep stream valleys, climb ridges to lookouts, and traverse the transition zone between field and forest where many species of birds and wildlife may be seen.

In the last century the valley attracted quite wealthy settlers and some trails lead to historic sites.

From the Governors Road entrance, the park road leads to a large parking lot, a short walk from the trail centre. This is located in a large Victorian reproduction of an old railroad station. The trail centre provides information and maps, as well as refreshments and washroom facilities.

Outside, on a short section of track that once was part of the Toronto, Hamilton and Buffalo railway, stands a large maroon executive coach that was built in 1929 and donated by Canadian Pacific Railways to the Conservation Authority in 1978, along with the 1931 baggage car beside it.

The Headwaters Trail is just one of a number of trails that radiate from the trail centre to all corners of the conservation area. Many may be combined for short or long loop trails.

The Headwaters Trail covered here, for example, traverses parts of the Bruce Trail, as well as the Lookout, Wilderness and Harvest trails. More loops may be added for a longer hike.

The trails are popular with both equestrians and cyclists and on nice days they tend to be busy close to the trail centre. The traffic thins out considerably when you get into the more remote parts of the conservation area.

The Headwaters Trail is blazed with a square symbol showing a stylized drawing of a valley and a flowing river. Be sure to follow this blaze when you leave the trail centre.

Leaving the trail centre, walk down the path and past the lawns to a gap in the trees on the other side of the railroad tracks. The Headwaters Trail crosses the railroad tracks and heads southward

Central Ontario

27

into a lovely hardwood forest where thick vines twine themselves around tree trunks and the raucous cry of a blue jay echoes through the woods. A white blaze signifies that this is a section of the Bruce Trail. The path is wide, with a gravel surface, and the terrain is undulating. After meandering through the forest it makes a sharp jog to the left over a dry stream bed, then eventually goes down a very steep slope to the valley cut by Sulphur Creek. If you look over to the right you will see Sulphur Springs Road. Beyond this is a spring that local settlers and aboriginal peoples used for its supposedly curative properties. In 1880, a nearby large house was turned into a hotel and spa and the fashionable came to take the waters. At times you can smell the sulphur that emanates from the spring as you follow the trail across the clear, sparkling creek.

On the other side of the creek the path starts into a steep climb up the escarpment using a series of wooden steps built into the bank. At the top, the trail branches off to the right, but before taking it, continue on the original trail just a few metres to have a look at the ruins of the Hermitage.

The Hermitage ruins are just that, ruins, but it is evident that this was once a house of some note. The few remaining walls are of locally quarried stone and there are a number of outbuilding foundations close to the original structure. The house was built in 1855 by George Leith, second son of a Scottish baronet, who owned a 100-ha farm here. No simple pioneer farmer, he filled his home with fine furniture from Scotland, valuable paintings and first-edition books, as well as employing five servants in the house. The Hermitage burned almost to the ground in 1934.

The Headwaters Trail skirts the north side of the Hermitage, goes through an opening in a rail fence and emerges onto wide lawns and a gravel driveway. Follow the driveway to the right for about 50 m, then watch for the path turning into the forest on your left. The path meanders through the woods a short way alongside a high ridge to your right. When you come to a sign that says Orchard Trail, the Headwaters Trail turns off to the right and heads up to the top of the ridge. On your way up you will notice to your left a huge uprooted tree. A red squirrel, its cheeks bulging with acorns, dashes across the path and behind a spaghetti-like curtain of roots into the cavernous hole left at the foot of the tree.

The trail reaches a gravel road and crosses it. The Homestead Trail, a 1-km trek that goes to a pretty waterfall, leads off to the right. Meanwhile, the Headwaters Trail leads up a grassy bank where the hedgerows are a tangle of raspberry bushes and grapes. Still climbing, the path comes out high above the busy Mineral Springs Road, descends and continues alongside for about 20 m, crosses it and enters the bush again through a gap in the fence.

The ecoystem changes here. The Carolinian forest gives way first to marshy lands where Joe pye-weed and cattails grow tall on each side of the path, and then to new growth of sumacs, blackberries and vines. In about 100 m the Headwaters Trail splits off to the left, crossing a short boardwalk. The Lookout Trail keeps straight and enters an incredibly dark, silent pine forest where the canopy is so thick it almost completely blots out the sun. After about 30 m the trail enters hardwoods again and the harsh scream of a red-tailed hawk resounds up and down the ridges. A climb up a long, steep hill brings you to the lookout where there is a seat. You have now been hiking about 70 minutes and have reached probably the best lunch spot on the trail.

The view to the south is spectacular over high forested hills. The trees here are alive with goldfinches and chattering chickadees. A black and white warbler flits into a pine tree.

The path continues down the other side of the ridge, turning a sharp left to rejoin the Headwaters Trail. The trail meanders on in a southerly direction and when it reaches an area of pines takes a sharp right. The Hilltop Trail, which intersects here, goes south.

The Headwaters Trail leads through a pine forest and shortly comes to a plank bridge over a little stream. The woods are quiet now, except for birds and the occasional squirrel, and there are few walkers. From the stream the path climbs a grassy hill and you can look behind and make out roughly the area where the seat on the Lookout Trail is located.

The trail passes through a reclaimed meadow on a path that has been cut through brushy undergrowth. It crosses Martin's Road and enters an area of tall white pines and old hardwoods, which eventually gives way to brush. The Tom Beckett Trail, which leads into a damp area of many springs, goes off to the left. After crossing

Sulphur Creek, the Headwaters Trail enters an area of lovely, forested high ridges. When you come to the junction with the Wilderness Trail, follow this new trail into an area of young trees, predominantly birch. After crossing another small stream, the two trails rejoin and enter a large marshy area where jewelweed grows in abundance.

The Headwaters Trail culminates in a climb up a long, winding hill up the escarpment. Turn right at the edge of a wheatfield and follow the Harvest Trail. This path runs between field and forest for about 2 km before looping back into the forest and rejoining the Headwaters Trail.

Aptly named, the Harvest Trail leads along cultivated fields, and past raspberry canes, elderberry and chokecherry, and a multitude of apple trees. After re-entering the forest and travelling downhill, the path comes into a large clearing where a garbage pail is chained to a tree. Turn right here, and travel about 800 m before meeting up with the Headwaters Trail and turning left to join it.

From here, for variety, continue on the Headwaters Trail through an area of high ridges and deep valleys instead of branching off to take the Wilderness Trail. If you wish to lengthen your walk, two other diversions can be taken on the way back. The Headwaters Trail passes the entrances to the Reforestation Trail and the G. Donald Trail, two short trails through replanted areas. Otherwise, follow the Headwaters Trail back to the trail centre.

Ganaraska Forest Centre

The Orange Trail

- **LENGTH:** 9 km (3 hours) • **DEGREE OF DIFFICULTY:** Easy
- **TYPE OF TRAIL:** Loop • **LOCATION:** Elizabethville

HOW TO GET THERE:

You can reach the Ganaraska Forest by following Highway 401, east of Bowmanville, exiting onto Highway 35. Drive north on Highway 35 to County Road 9, then turn east towards Bewdley. After passing through the village of Kendal, watch for Ganaraska Forest Centre signs and turn left, following the signs to the Centre parking lot.

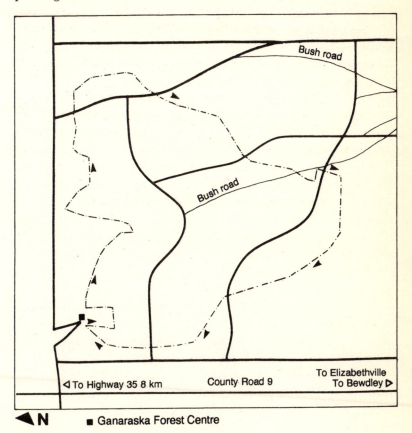

◄ N   ■ Ganaraska Forest Centre

The Ganaraska Forest is a good place for a walk in the woods. It is lovely in spring when the forest floor is carpeted with trilliums and the trees are noisy with new life. The chirruping of black and white warblers is overpowered by the raucous cry of a blue jay, but your heart almost stops when a ruffed grouse bursts cover next to your boots. The one drawback is rampant poison ivy, but it is avoidable with care.

The 43,000-ha forest is operated by the Ganaraska Region Conservation Authority. Many of the trails in the Forest Centre are managed for ski trails in the winter. The Central Sector of the forest has some 30 km of trails, but other trails follow logging roads that penetrate deep into the bush in both the East and West Sectors. You could walk for days in this place.

The Ganaraska Forest is pleasantly situated on the rolling hills of the Oak Ridges Moraine, a ridge of high sandy hills north of Toronto that was formed by two retreating glacier arms. The Ganaraska occupies the northeastern section of the moraine.

Almost all of this magnificent forest was planted. The soils are thin—almost pure sand—so when pioneer farmers cleared the land for agriculture, winds piled the sand into dunes and so eroded the land it became a desert. In the 1940s the Conservation Authority bought the land and began a planting program. Today it represents one of the most successful regeneration and rehabilitation efforts in Ontario.

The trails in the Ganaraska Forest Centre are some of the best marked anywhere, mainly for the convenience of hundreds of cross-country skiers. The Orange Trail is a new addition and is the second longest single trail in the Forest Centre. All are loop trails, although there is a linear trail to an old fire tower, which takes about 4 hours total to complete.

The trail system starts from a parking lot that serves the Forest Centre. A cluster of low buildings here functions as school facilities for the six school boards that use the centre for educational purposes.

Here, also, a large grassy area, surrounded by lovely, towering white pines offers a picnic spot for pre- or post-trail relaxing. A couple of pit toilets are the only washroom facilities.

To access the trail, cross the grassy area and head northwards through an opening in the forest. The Orange Trail, naturally, is designated by orange markers on the trees. It shares part of the way with the Blue Trail.

The trail meanders up hill and down as it winds through the forest. The path is wide and it is a good idea not to stray from it as there are few points of reference and numerous confusing pathways.

The forest environment changes every 250 m or so. The path leads through plantations where pines march like soldiers over sandy soils. Next comes a hardwood bush where there is thick, luxuriant undergrowth. Then the trail passes through mixed forest until it again reaches a pine plantation, and the process starts over again as the path winds through the varied forest sectors.

A thick layer of pine needles cushions the path as you walk and there are enough hills to give you a bit of a workout. Here and there boulders lay dumped just as the glacier left them, and the farming history of the area is evident in scattered piles of stones. The smell of pine boughs compares with the world's most expensive perfume.

The forest is alive with sounds of birds and the chattering of chipmunks. It is remarkably shy of human sounds, even though multiple-use trails cross and intersect with hiking trails. When you have been hiking about 1 hour the trail crosses a bush road and you will see a swampy area on your right. The trail crosses at the end of the swamp and it can be very wet here. A little farther along, a loop called the "B" Trail takes off to the left while the Orange Trail continues downhill. At this point, the Orange Trail starts heading back, but don't fall into the trap of thinking you are halfway home; the longest part of the trail still remains.

The trail so far has been meandering north, and gently but steadily rising up the slopes of the Oak Ridges Moraine. Numerous sandy ridges give the forest some character.

Now the trail heads east and south, and generally downwards. Here and there look for some huge old white pines that must be the only survivors of the original forest.

About 2 km from the trail end you get the walk's only real view. Here, where the remains of a pioneer orchard stabilize a slope, is a marvellous view of the Oak Ridges Moraine to the west. You can see the topmost ridges, the fire tower and the rolling forested hills that march to the top of the moraine.

The Ganaraska Forest is an example of multiple use that offers many recreational opportunities. There are many kilometres of unmapped trails that you can take advantage of if you prefer to walk in either the West or East Sectors. The 200-km Ganaraska Trail winds through part of the East Sector. Be warned, however, that hunting is allowed in those areas, in season.

There is no charge for use of the trails.

Hockley Valley

Bruce Trail

- **LENGTH**: 12 km (4 hours) • **DEGREE OF DIFFICULTY**: Moderate
- **TYPE OF TRAIL**: Loop • **LOCATION**: Orangeville

HOW TO GET THERE:

This trail is accessed from the Hockley Valley Road, 5 km east of Highway 10, north of Orangeville. There is a small parking area on both sides of the Hockley Valley Road, just west of the village of Glen Cross. Look for Bruce Trail blazes on the north side of the road, where the trail starts.

• • •

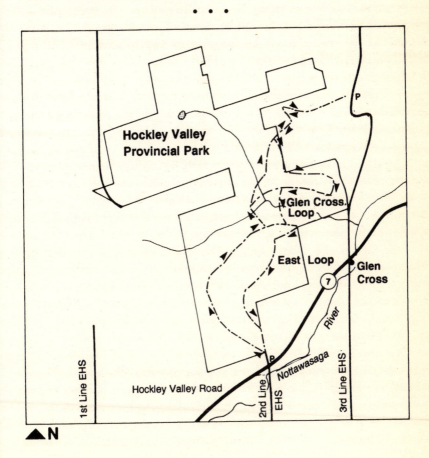

An attractive and convenient loop using Bruce Trail side trails makes for a lovely walk in the Hockley Valley. It is a particularly good fall walk because it can be hot work negotiating the many hills. In fall hardwood forests dress the hills in spectacular colours, and brilliant scarlet sumacs light up the meadows. A loop hike that includes travel on the Hockley Valley Road and on the 3rd Line EHS is also popular with hikers.

The Hockley Valley is part of the Niagara Escarpment, although the prominent cliffs that are such distinctive features of this landform are not present here. Instead, this is an area of steep wooded hillsides and narrow valleys intersected by watercourses. The most notable of these is the Nottawasaga River which meanders over its bed of stones on the valley floor. The trail involves some fairly steep climbs and descents which can be very slippery in wet weather. The valley owes its beauty to ancient receding glaciers that mounded gravel into moraines resulting in many small hills and valleys.

There is parking space for about ten cars on either side of the Hockley Valley Road. The trail, marked by white blazes on the north side of the road, goes up a sandy bank and into the trees and starts a long climb, passing some boulders. In about 200 m the trail splits and a side trail which you will return on carries on up a road allowance. The main trail takes a swing to the left.

You are now in Hockley Valley Provincial Park which is as yet unregulated so no services are offered. Still climbing, the path goes through open meadows until it reaches the top of a ridge. Behind you, across the valley, you can see the ski trails of the Hockley Valley Ski Resort cutting a green swath down the valley sides. From the ridge, the trail enters a mature hardwood forest and continues in an undulating fashion up, over, and down a multitude of small hills. After about 2 km the trail joins some old logging roads and veers eastward, emerging onto a trail that runs parallel to the Nottawasaga River.

When you come to an intersection of trails you have a choice of returning via the East Loop and cutting your trip roughly in half, or continuing northwards following the main Bruce Trail to hook up with the Glen Cross Loop at its northernmost point.

The main trail turns left and descends a slope into the valley made by the Nottawasaga and crosses the river. There is a steep climb out of the valley to the top of the slope. The path continues over forested ridges and winds around another incline and through a cedar bush before descending a steep slope to cross a plank bridge over a large stream. It is muddy through here after spring rains.

The trail zigzags up and over the next ridge where it meets the southern terminus of the Glen Cross Loop, which winds off to the east following blue trail signs.

The main trail, following white blazes, continues northwards up and over numerous forested hills in a switchback fashion. Deep valleys carved by glaciers fall away to the side. The path is so well established on this part of the Bruce Trail that you will not need to watch for trail signs for most of the way. The trail arrives at another large stream that sparkles in the sunlight, making riffles as it crosses a series of small boulders. Across the stream, the path continues up a long, steep hill as it travels northward through hardwood forest.

At the top of the hill there is a double blue blaze signifying the Snell Loop, a short trail that goes off to the left. A few steps farther on will bring you to the northern arm of the Glen Cross Loop. At this point you can choose to turn right onto the Glen Cross Loop and start your return trip. However, it is worth while to continue northwards about another 1 km because it is a nice walk. If you do continue, you will need to return to this point via the same path.

Continuing in a generally northeast direction, the path crosses another small, clear stream, then travels alongside it for some 300 m. If you stop here for lunch you can pick watercress from the stream to spice up your sandwich.

From the stream the path climbs a high sandy ridge on the right to a pine plantation, from where there are views to the south and northwest. The trail ends a few metres farther on, so this is a good place to turn around and retrace your steps to the first arm of the Glen Cross Loop.

Back at the point where the Glen Cross Loop intersects the main trail, the loop leads off to the left. It goes south for about 250 m, then turns sharply eastward to the eastern boundary of the provincial park. The path goes through the forest and down into a meadow in a deep valley. At the bottom of the meadow the path veers roughly westwards and crosses a pretty little stream. It then passes through a wood before entering a large meadow where a narrow path cuts through tall grass. When the path enters the forest again, look for a double blaze on a tree and make a sharp turn southwards along a grassy, muddy path. Look carefully for blazes; this section is not well signed.

The path leads through a marshy area bordering both sides of the Nottawasaga River and crosses the river by means of a log bridge. The trail turns left at an intersection of paths and parallels a shallow stream. It crosses the stream and rises to higher ground before making a sharp right turn and following a laneway. Again, watch carefully for blazes.

Approximately 300 m along the laneway you will come to a stile which leads into a meadow. Cross the stile and continue to the right along the fenceline, then follow the well-worn path to the

Hockley Valley

top of a very steep incline. Bird boxes dot the meadow. If you turn around there are lovely, long views of the rolling hills to the north.

At the top of the hill, cross another stile and turn left. The path now runs through a forested area and up and down numerous steep inclines for about 1 km until it joins the main trail a few metres from the Hockley Valley Road.

Mono Cliffs

- **LENGTH:** 6 km (2.5 hours)
- **DEGREE OF DIFFICULTY:** Easy to moderate
- **TYPE OF TRAIL:** Loop • **LOCATION:** Mono Centre

HOW TO GET THERE:

Take Highways 10/24 about 7 km north of Orangeville. Turn east onto Regional Road 8 at Camilla and follow the 2nd Line EHS north to Mono Centre. Continue north of the village on the 2nd Line EHS to the parking lot. There are no fees for hiking in this park.

• • •

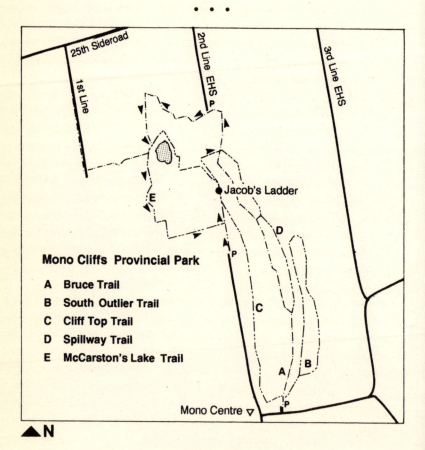

Mono Cliffs Provincial Park

A   Bruce Trail
B   South Outlier Trail
C   Cliff Top Trail
D   Spillway Trail
E   McCarston's Lake Trail

We discovered the trails of Mono Cliffs Provincial Park on the first day of spring when winter had not yet released its grip. It was beautiful in its pristine whiteness. The trails here can be enjoyed any time of year, but fall is especially lovely when maples and beeches garb themselves for a last, glorious exotic fling before assuming the sombre mantle of winter.

The 750-ha park is another in a series of parks that protect the dramatic southern Ontario landform of unsurpassing beauty that is the Niagara Escarpment. The Bruce Trail passes through the park and a number of park trails loop and interconnect allowing you to suit your walk to your particular mood.

Prime attractions are long views and walks through mixed and hardwood forests, as well as a walk along the base of tall cliffs. For those interested in geological history, there are two prominent outliers, a glacial spillway and a kame moraine and crevice caves. Among the 450 plant species are rare ferns. The trails range from a 500 m descent of the escarpment to the approximately 6-km round trip detailed here.

This trail is a longer version of the McCarston's Lake Trail which starts at the south parking lot on the 2nd Line, 2 km north of the village of Mono Centre.

The trail follows the line of the escarpment north, then joins the Cliff Top Trail which leads to the phenomenon known as Jacob's Ladder. Past Jacob's Ladder, the McCarston's Lake Trail leads off to the left, but ignore this and take the right fork that leads down the escarpment to join the main Bruce Trail. By following the Bruce Trail north you can walk underneath the overhanging talus cliffs and marvel at the old cedars clinging to the rockface. Best of all, you can make your way to one of the highest points in the park, which offers fantastic long views.

The trail starts in the northeast corner of the parking lot and follows a laneway downhill. To the left are fields and to the right wooded lands stretch to the edge of the escarpment. About 80 m along, a lane leads to the left, which will be your point of exit on the return trip. Do not turn left onto the laneway.

Continue down the path and it will suddenly become very apparent that you are close to the cliff edge. This part is fenced. Through the trees you can see the flat valley floor and the rising

South Outlier, a piece of the escarpment which has broken off from the main scarp. The trail joins here with the Cliff Top Trail, which is characterized by a blue marker. Follow these blue markers. There is a good view here of the rolling lands that stretch many miles eastward.

Soon you will arrive at Jacob's Ladder where you can stand on the viewing platform and look down the face of the escarpment. A set of steps leads down the cliff face and into a deep fissure. The rock here was the base of a large inland sea 400 million years ago and the fossilized remains of some of the sea creatures are part of the rock face. The rock face itself is rugged with crevice caves, chimneys and slopes formed of falling rocks. Stunted trees cling to the rock face and rare ferns and mosses grow among the fallen rocks at the base of the cliff.

Continuing north on the trail you will come to another fork. The trail that goes directly to McCarston's Lake veers off to the left, but we will follow the Spillway Trail, which angles around an ancient many-limbed beech tree and heads downhill to the right.

The path here winds through a lovely mixed forest and the branches form a canopy overhead. Look closely at some of the trees here and you will see the large square holes that are made by the pileated woodpecker.

At the bottom of the hill the path joins the Bruce Trail and swings north again climbing a seemingly never-ending hill. To the right, according to the park brochure, the flat lands are the glacial spillway that was formed by the great retreating glacier. The views improve as you climb. To the south you will see the foundation of a pioneer farm and wonder at the toughness of those who tried to wrest a living from this land.

The path leads on towards the north parking lot and it is necessary here to pay attention to the trail signs because the trail is somewhat confusing. Follow the trail through the south end of the lot and veer towards the southwest. About 90 m farther on you will climb to one of the highest points in the park. The views are outstanding to the south, east and west. Beneath you are the treetops of a hardwood forest.

The trail then heads northwest and into a hardwood forest, before dipping sharply south once again. It then leads to a point where it converges with the McCarston's Lake Trail. You will need to pay attention here and look for the yellow hiking signs or you may find yourself heading out of the park as it follows the Bruce Trail north to Tobermory.

Below you lies the pretty kettle lake that gives the trail its name. This is a lovely shady spot for a picnic lunch. Skirt the lake to the right and continue on south through the forest until you come to a fence where the trail forks once again. Take the turn to the right around a field where you will see a bluebird box. This will lead to a cart track and you will turn left and follow this about 250 m to where it joins the Cliff Top Trail leading to the parking lot.

Mount Nemo

Bruce Trail

- **LENGTH:** 11 km (4 hours)
- **DEGREE OF DIFFICULTY:** Easy to moderate
- **TYPE OF TRAIL:** Linear • **LOCATION:** Burlington

HOW TO GET THERE:

Take Highway 401 to Interchange 312, south on Regional Road 1, (Guelph Line) 15 km to Colling Road. If car jockeying, leave one

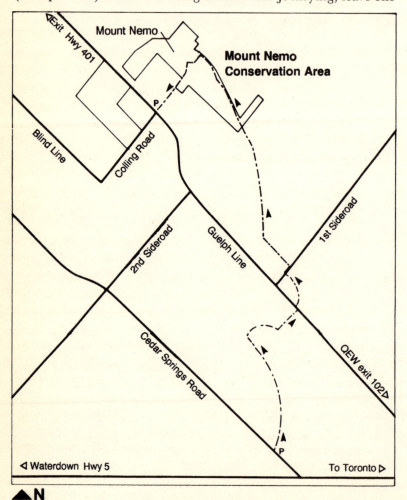

car on Colling Road and take the other south on Guelph Line to Highway 5, then west on Highway 5 to Cedar Springs Road, north about 250 m on Cedar Springs Road. Park on the shoulder. Look for a yellow pole on the east side of the road, where the trail starts.

• • •

This trail ascends the bluff known as Mount Nemo, long known as one of the best viewpoints in the Toronto–Hamilton area. From this promontory, part of the Niagara Escarpment, there are stunning panoramic views of the southern Ontario plains on the northern shores of Lake Ontario. To the north can be seen the Milton Outlier, familiarly known as Rattlesnake Point. On clear days, hikers can see the CN Tower in Toronto's downtown. It is gorgeous on a sunny fall day when the waters of Lake Ontario make a lovely blue border for glorious autumn colours.

Mount Nemo is a popular destination for spelunkers as well as hikers. The spelunkers come to explore the system of vertical caves and crevices, which are a habitat for various species of bats. The crevices were created from water flowing through the rocks thousands of years ago. Although not large, they are numerous, allowing spelunkers to crawl many hundreds of metres under the escarpment. People are cautioned not to try this unless accompanied by a skilled spelunker or someone who is very familiar with the area.

The Halton Region Conservation Authority acquired the property some 32 years ago when it was realized that a nearby quarry operation had plans to break through the face of the bluff. Soon after this acquisition, a provincial committee was formed to discuss the significance of the natural phenomenon known as the Niagara Escarpment. Some 15 years later, the Niagara Escarpment Plan was approved to protect this precious southern Ontario resource. It may be argued, therefore, that Mount Nemo was a catalyst in preserving the Niagara Escarpment we have today.

The trail detailed here follows the long, southern approach to the top of Mount Nemo, but two of the major lookouts may be accessed by a short walk from the Guelph Line, so hikers who take this longer route may find the area quite busy when they reach the bluff near the end of their hike.

From Cedar Springs Road, the trail follows a gradual incline to the top of the escarpment, following it in a northerly direction before swinging westwards, passing some caves and then finally heading south to Colling Road.

This is an excellent way to climb the escarpment because the incline is gradual and there is very little hard climbing involved. From Cedar Springs Road, the trail climbs the bank on the north side of the road near a yellow pole on which is painted the familiar white blaze of the Bruce Trail. Following a wellworn path it enters an area of scrub brush where clusters of blushing wild apples and patches of goldenrod, fleabane and New England aster add splashes of colour. The trail winds up and down this reclaimed meadow for some 400 m before entering a mature forest that glows with the varied reds, bronzes and coppers of fall hardwoods. Climbing steadily up the escarpment, the trail meanders through hardwood forest over numerous ridges and through small ravines. These may be damp and soggy following wet weather. After crossing another open, overgrown meadow the trail goes over a bridge, turns left and climbs a hill.

From here it enters an open, rolling area from where there are good views of the lake and the sprawling city of Burlington to the south.

At the end of the field, the trail crosses a gravel path that leads to a large house on the far left, then crosses a stream to enter a hardwood forest. There are few experiences more pleasant than a tramp through woods such as these on a fall day. The trail travels under a canopy of brilliant fall colour, dry leaves crackle underfoot and the silence is broken only by the echoing call of a blue jay.

The trail climbs steadily up through the forest until it emerges at the edge of a cornfield where it turns right. After a few paces it enters an overgrown meadow where chickadees and blue jays call from a tall hedgerow rampant with wild grapes and brilliant red crab-apples. The path meanders over the meadow until it reaches a pond on the left side of the trail. A blue heron fishes unconcernedly for food in the shallows. The trail skirts the pond and turns around the end of it, then climbs a hill leading to a forested valley of beautiful old beeches and maples. The trail zigzags through here climbing steadily and turns right at the top of the valley. It then crosses a stream and skirts the edge of a ploughed field until it reaches Guelph Line.

After crossing Guelph Line the trail turns left for about 150 m before turning right at the white blaze. This takes you into a cornfield that is bordered by a colourful hedgerow of sumac and apple trees. The walking here is poor, especially following wet weather, because there is no defined path. Follow the hedgerow to the end of the field and enter a mostly hardwood bush dotted with young white pines, cross a stream, climb a hill and emerge onto the 1st Sideroad.

Turn right onto the sideroad and go about 40 m, then turn left through a gateway into an old orchard that has a bountiful harvest of wild apples and pears and sour chokecherries. This is about the half-way point of the trail and a good spot for lunch.

From the orchard the trail continues a steady climb up to the escarpment and here the views become spectacular. Below, stretching south and east, are orchards and cornfields, farms and villages, and beyond them the communities that make up Canada's most populated area.

The trail follows the top of the escarpment for about 5 km, passing the edge of a fence around the grounds of a large house. From here it crosses a field and enters another forest before reaching the top of Mount Nemo where there are numerous lookouts.

The rocky terrain is slashed every which way with deep fissures, some of which lead to the vertical caves. In some of Mount Nemo's shady, limestone crevices grows the rare hart's-tongue fern. A little way along, a side trail goes off to the right and down the escarpment to join Walkers Line near the Indian Wells Golf Course.

Continuing along the top of Mount Nemo, the trail reaches a cement-enclosed lookout constructed by the Halton Region Conservation Authority, then turns a sharp left to follow a road allowance back to the parking area on Colling Road.

Alternatively, you can continue along the top of Mount Nemo past another Halton Region Conservation Authority Lookout and an area of more caves. This trail then swings left, passing under some power lines and following an old quarry road to Guelph Line near Colling Road. This will add another 3 km to your hike.

Oak Ridges Moraine Trail

Durham Regional Forest and Glen Major Conservation Area

- **LENGTH:** 13 km (4 hours) • **DEGREE OF DIFFICULTY:** Easy
- **TYPE OF TRAIL:** Linear (loops available) • **LOCATION:** Uxbridge

HOW TO GET THERE:

The trail starts southeast of Uxbridge. Take Durham Regional Road 23 to Pinegate Road, just south of Regional Road 21 and park on the shoulder. If car jockeying, park the second car on the shoulder of Lakeridge Road, 4 km south on Regional Road 23, west side, just past the Dagmar Ski Area entrance. To access the

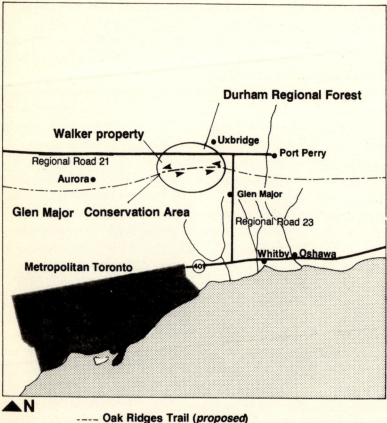

▲N

- - - - **Oak Ridges Trail (proposed)**

◯ **Uxbridge Area Trails and Durham Forest**

Hiking Ontario's Heartland

trail from Pinegate Road, cross Regional Road 23 and walk north about 100 m to the entrance to the Durham Regional Forest.

• • •

An Oak Ridges Moraine trail that stretches some 160 km across the top of the Greater Toronto area is a dream in the making. Until it becomes a reality, hikers can use numerous trails on public lands dotted along its expanse. These are not well known, except for those in Conservation Areas such as the Albion Hills. Trails on other public lands, such as those in the Durham Regional Forest, are being mapped and marked as resources permit. Before hiking them, it would be useful to contact the Metro Toronto and Region Conservation Authority, or Hike Ontario! to enquire about the existence of a trail map. Otherwise, a topographic map and compass would be an asset to negotiating a confusing network of paths and old logging roads.

The Oak Ridges Moraine is one of the most prominent landforms in southern Ontario. Stretching between the Niagara Escarpment and the Trent River in Peterborough, it provides a major recreational resource for people living in the southern Ontario Golden Horseshoe area.

The moraine was formed during the last ice age when melting glaciers deposited mounds of glacial drift material—mainly sand, gravel and silt. The result is a picturesque hilly area lying just north of Toronto, from where there are panoramic views of the flat plain covered by the sprawl of Metropolitan Toronto and its satellite communities.

It contains the headwaters of more than 30 rivers that drain into Lake Ontario in the south and Lake Simcoe in the north. This makes it an important source of drinking water for the millions living in this heavily populated area. It is ideal hiking country. Rolling, hummocky hills make excellent lookout points and add interest to the trail. In its valleys, where deer herds flourish, it is possible to feel far removed from the teeming streets of nearby urban centres.

A major east-west trail along the moraine that would link the Bruce Trail in the west with the Ganaraska in the east is the goal of the Oak Ridges Trail Association. The group is working towards opening the trail, section by section, along this natural and beautiful corridor.

The stretch covered here travels through the pines of the Durham Regional Forest, and enters the 429-ha Walker property that was acquired by the Metropolitan Toronto and Region Conservation Authority in 1991. It then enters the Glen Major Conservation Area, where it leaves the forest and emerges onto open hills that offer long views to the south. Travelling by a little-used gravel road, it crosses Duffin Creek before ending near the Dagmar Ski Area. This trail requires car jockeying, but a network of trails in the forest allows for some creative loop hikes.

After entering the Durham Regional Forest, the trail follows a wide sandy roadway through a reclaimed meadow planted with young pine. Follow the path as it veers north, paralleling Regional Road 23. The meadow is colourful with New England aster, milkweed, butter and eggs, Queen Anne's lace, goldenrod and mullein.

The path swings west after about 100 m and enters a pine plantation, still following the wide, well-defined path. The floor is loosely packed sand, but not difficult to walk on. The forest floor under the pines is lush with bracken fern. Where the sun hits the opening on each side of the road, juicy, sweet blackberries grow in profusion, along with black-eyed Susans and evening primrose. The land is gently undulating.

When you come to a tree marked ''Route 125'' where there is a path going off to the right, pass it and keep straight on. This is the first of many similar paths that intersect the forest and it is easy to become confused.

When you reach the end of this path at a T-junction, you will have walked about 2 km. Take the left fork, heading roughly southeast. After about 500 m you will come to a long hill with an open, grassy area at the top. From the grassy area you can see a microwave tower at the top of another hill. Walk past the tower and cross the 7th Concession, Uxbridge, then enter through an orange metal gate. You are now walking adjacent to the Walker property, which is on your left.

The Walker property, part of the headwaters of Duffin Creek, was once a barren wasteland. Over a space of 57 years, James

Walker, his wife Olwen, and a few staff and volunteers planted more than two million trees to return the land to forest and protect it from erosion. It was acquired by the Metro Toronto Conservation Authority in July, 1991, and to date, while it may be used by hikers, there is no official access, nor parking.

A short walk along the wide path brings you to a hill from where there are excellent views of rolling, grassy knolls backed by forested hills. The road goes downhill and enters a hardwood forest. About 500 m after leaving the gate, look for a small opening in the fence on the left. Squeeze through this and turn right when you reach the path. You are now on the Walker property. The path here is on loosely packed sandy loam, which makes walking difficult. Large, fresh deer tracks are numerous.

At the first turning, follow the path left into the forest. The walking is better now on hard-packed earth but the forest is a maze of paths that are impossible to keep track of without a topographic map, or enlarged aerial photograph. Both of these items are obtainable from the Public Information Centre of the Ontario Ministry of Natural Resources in Toronto at the address given in the Appendix. Staff will assist you to order the appropriate map or photograph.

The trail twists and turns through the forest, which changes from pine stands to mixed hardwoods, where there are a number of large old oaks. It passes close to the fence line alongside private property where you will notice a lovely old log church that has been converted into a home.

At the bottom of a long hill, a large, grassy clearing ringed by white pines makes an ideal lunch stop. You are now in the Glen Major Conservation Area. From here, the trail heads back up the hill and heads east, then south, eventually abandoning the wide, well-used tracks in favour of narrow paths through the hardwoods. The forest floor reveals interesting fungi, jewelweed and may-apple. Working our way south, we left the path altogether at the bottom of a hill, following a fence line over a ridge. After climbing another hill we emerged onto a wide grassy opening with many small, rolling hills. A worn pathway to the east leads to the top of a high hill offering marvellous panoramic views to the south and west.

The path continues across reclaimed meadows up and down over gravelly hills for about 500 m before entering a shady forest. Emerging from the forest, the trail re-crosses the 7th Concession and continues along Lakeridge Road, a sideroad on the east side that leads to Dagmar Ski Area. The sideroad parallels Duffin Creek for a short way, then crosses it and starts to ascend an enormously long, winding hill that leads to the lifts. The trail ends about 100 m east of the ski lifts.

Primrose and the Boyne River Valley

Bruce Trail Loop

- **LENGTH:** 14 km (5 hours)
- **DEGREE OF DIFFICULTY:** Easy to moderate
- **TYPE OF TRAIL:** Loop • **LOCATION:** East of Shelburne

HOW TO GET THERE:

The trail starts on the 1st Line WHS, 1.5 km north of the village of Primrose, which lies at the junction of Highway 10/24 and Highway 89. The 1st Line WHS runs north from Highway 10/24 when that highway swings west toward Shelburne. There is a small parking area on the east side of the 1st Line WHS, next to a bridge

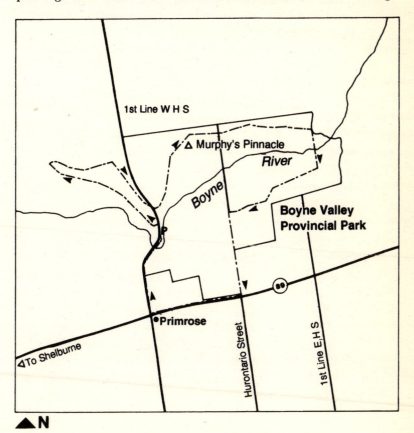

over the Boyne River. The loop hike includes walking about 1 km along busy Highway 89. This can be avoided if you are in a two-car party as one car can be left on the shoulder of Highway 89 east of Primrose where the trail emerges.

• • •

This trail boasts two attractions. One high point is literally a high point—Murphy's Pinnacle. This is a grassy hill from which there is a commanding view of the rolling countryside to the south, west and east. The second attraction is a walk through the lovely, verdant, narrow valley of the Boyne River.

After parking on 1st Line WHS, walk north on the sideroad and down the hill until you see the ruins of an old house on the east side. Cross to the west side and look for a sign that says "Provincial Park." A blue blaze shows the direction of the path which leads upwards through a cedar forest. As you climb you can see lovely views of forested hills and the Boyne River below.

The trail skirts the edge of a pine forest and then enters it. The path keeps a straight course for 50 m or so and then twists to the left. When it starts to go right again, keep your eyes open for a tree on your right that carries the double blaze sign indicating a turn in the trail. This turn is very obscure and easily missed. Once you have made the turn, the trail is very well marked with blue blazes on just about every other tree.

After following a straight line for about 500 m, the trail makes a sharp right turn into a deep, dark wood. The silence is shattered by the cry of a blue jay that resents intrusion into its domain. About 500 m along, look for a turn to the left where the trail leaves the forest and enters a meadow. Skirting a hill, the trail crosses a pile of stones and eventually becomes a grassy track that winds uphill between scattered cedars. This is a good spot to watch for deer, judging by the amount of droppings. Hills may be seen to the west.

The trail continues to climb, crossing a series of small ridges. Watch for it branching and take the branch that veers to the left and goes downhill, crossing a small gully. Old apple trees grow among the cedars and small pines. This appears to be pioneer farming country that is regenerating to its original forest.

Still climbing, the trail comes to a junction with a cart track.

Turn right onto this cart track and continue southwards through mature pines. There are blackberry bushes galore around here. The cart track culminates in a grassy meadow and when it does, look to your left just before reaching a clump of old willows. There must have been an old farmhouse here because, in season, the place is rampant with old-fashioned roses that carry a perfume modern roses do not seem to have.

(A snowmobile trail turns left here, skirts the old farmsite, crosses a stream and shortly emerges onto the 1st Line WHS. However, this will put you on the sideroad north of where the trail continues on the east side of the 1st Line WHS.)

To continue on the main trail, look for a blue blaze on an old apple tree to your right and follow the trail along a fern-edged path into the pine forest. Soon you will see the 1st Line WHS running alongside to the left. You are now walking through mixed bush. Watch carefully for a double blaze showing a turn to the left. It is not well marked.

Turning left at the trail fork leads you into a lovely, shady wood high above the road. The path descends very quickly and steeply to emerge onto the sideroad. Look to the right across the road to where there is a road sign (arrow). A double blue blaze is painted on the pole beneath the sign. The trail leads behind a small mound of gravel.

You will now have been walking 1 hour and are about 200 m north of the parking lot where you started your walk.

The next leg of the trail rises to Murphy's Pinnacle. From the 1st Line WHS, the path climbs slowly but steadily upwards through a mature maple forest. At the top, look for a double blaze on a tree to your left and follow the well-worn path downhill. At the bottom is a large bed of graceful ostrich fern. The path twists, turns, and climbs a hill until it comes to a stile. You can now see Murphy's Pinnacle, a grass-covered drumlin that appears to be the highest point of land in this area. You can just make out the path as it winds upwards.

Cross the stile and follow the fence line to your left, staying close to it again at the top of the field. It is a long climb that offers panoramic views of this rural Ontario countryside. Rolling hills dotted with farms and forests stretch to the east and south, and to the west you can see across the fields to the town of Shelburne. Trees to the north obscure the view of the Mulmur Hills. This is one of the two best lunch stops on the trail. The other is on a hill almost directly south of Murphy's Pinnacle, about a 90-minute walk from here.

The path follows the top of the ridge, carpeted with yellow and orange hawkweed and trefoil. Then it goes in an easterly direction underneath another hill that is blue with spikes of viper's bugloss. Blue markers on stones denote the trail which leads towards a fence. Do not cross the fence. Turn right alongside it and follow the fence line down the hill and into a meadow that is turning back to bush.

At the bottom of the field, cross a stile and you will emerge onto a farm laneway, which is actually Hurontario Street, the old main pioneer highway. The sideroads in this area are named EHS or WHS because they are either east, or west, of Hurontario Street.

Cross Hurontario Street and look almost immediately for the path leading off to the right where there is a double blaze. A provincial park sign indicates that you are now leaving public land and entering private land. The owners have granted permission for hikers to cross their land, but be sure to stay on the established path, especially in planted areas or hayfields.

After turning right, the path follows a farm track through a regenerating meadow. You will pass an old cabin or farm out-building and then along the edge of a couple of fields.

From here, the path enters a wood, rich with ostrich ferns, wild-flowers and wild rhubarb, and goes down into a ravine. An enormous old beech sends gnarled, distorted limbs skyward. Just past this, look for a double blaze and turn left, descending some wooden steps into a marshy area where there is a boardwalk.

On the other side of the boardwalk the trail enters another wood where there are huge old maples, and a stream running to your right. You are now walking through a lovely, deep, narrow ravine. Filtered sunlight dapples ferns and wildflowers that carpet the narrow valley floor. A surprised deer springs up the steep, wooded hillside.

The main Bruce Trail separates from the side trail here, climbing the steep hillside to the left. Our trail continues along the valley floor, eventually emerging onto the 1st Line EHS.

Hiking Ontario's Heartland

Turn right and follow this sideroad about 1 km, crossing the Boyne River. When you come to a long "S" turn, and just before climbing a long hill, you will see a double blaze and a Bruce Trail sign on the right. This leads into a tunnel-like archway of cedars with the proverbial light at the end of it where it emerges into an opening.

This path winds through woods and up some fairly steep hills. At the summit you can picnic at a point from where you can look north to the bald, rounded hill that is Murphy's Pinnacle. Below, forested hills hide the Boyne Valley.

Follow the blue signs across rolling meadowland and climb a long, gentle slope. At the top, look for a gap in the rail fence to your right. Turn left onto the Hurontario Street road allowance and follow the road allowance perhaps 1 km to where it emerges onto Highway 89.

At Highway 89, turn right, keeping to the shoulder until you get to the village of Primrose, then turn north and walk 1.5 km on the 1st Line WHS to the parking lot.

Seaton Trail

• **LENGTH:** 10 km (3+ hours) • **DEGREE OF DIFFICULTY:** Easy
• **TYPE OF TRAIL:** Linear • **LOCATION:** Pickering

HOW TO GET THERE:

This trail runs between Rossland Road in the south to Highway 7 in the north. It may also be accessed from Whitevale Road or Taunton Road. To reach Rossland Road, take Exit 399 on the 401 and drive the Brock Road north to Rossland Road (first left north of Finch). Turn west onto Rossland Road to parking area at Camp Pidaca. The Highway 7 access point is just east of Pickering Townline Road on the south side.

• • •

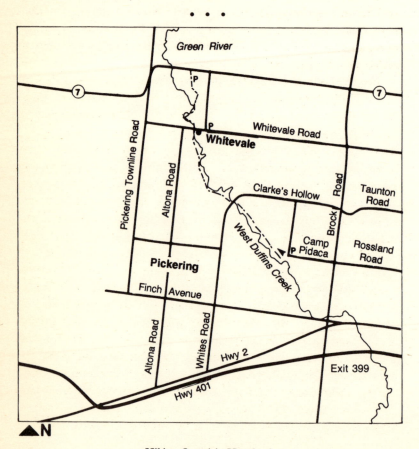

Hiking Ontario's Heartland

This trail runs through the valley of the West Duffins Creek, just north of its junction with the East Branch, on the final leg of the creek's journey to Lake Ontario. The valley is of enormous worth to residents living in the eastern portion of Metropolitan Toronto because it is a natural oasis almost on their doorsteps. Hikers can travel this natural corridor over more than 404 ha of public land and enjoy a link with nature not far from city streets.

The valley's first users were First Nations peoples who harvested salmon from the creek and game from the valley. Later, pioneers built several water-powered mills, which generated a thriving economic community. A grist mill still exists in the village of Whitevale on the upper part of the trail. The rest have disappeared and nature has restored the valley to a natural sanctuary of reclaimed meadows, marshy lands and wooded slopes. In small pockets are remnants of the forest that stood here before the arrival of the pioneers. These are old maple and beech trees, some of them perhaps 400 years old.

The trail was created by the Metropolitan Toronto and Region Conservation Authority on land owned by the Ontario Land Corporation. High school and university students employed on an Ontario summer works program marked and cleared it.

It is divided into three sections, two of which incorporate short loops, making an interesting diversion if you are hiking one section both ways. The three trails are the Heritage Trail, the Wilderness Trail and the Walking Trail. The self-interpreting trails are designed to introduce the hiker to the natural and historic features of the area. They are marked with yellow blazes.

The Heritage Trail occupies the most northerly section, running southward from Green River to Whitevale, a distance of almost 2.5 km one way. A loop roughly in the middle of this section circles around both the east and west banks, as well as the pond formed by the old pioneer dam. Starting from Highway 7 the path follows an old laneway on the east side of the valley for a little more than 1 km before crossing the creek to the West Circuit. Near the crossing look for an old white pine trunk. A little farther on exercise caution around the deep holes caused by water erosion in the banks.

The path travels south through cedar and hemlock woods where there are interesting ferns, then on through an old orchard. Soon you will come to the edge of a large pond that was created 100 years ago when the creek was dammed. Marshy areas around the pond are spanned by log bridges. At the southern edge of the pond is the old dam site. The dam was built to hold back the water, allowing it to be channelled into the mill. The dam powered the mill until 1974. The waterwheel used by the mill is still there and you will see this a little farther downstream.

This first section of the trail ends at the village of Whitevale. You can return using the East Circuit and perhaps stop and explore some of the pondlife en route.

The middle section of the trail is the Wilderness Trail and it runs almost 4 km from Whitevale south to Clarkes Hollow. In this more remote section of the trail are remnants of ancient forest and hidden groves of hemlock. Wild grape vines drape themselves over trees and shrubs, and deer, birds and other wildlife species find homes in the valley. Heading south on the east side of the creek the trail passes through a cedar swamp where there are colonies of ferns. About 500 m farther on there is an area of severe bank erosion. The trail continues over a living cedar bridge and eventually to a lookout. An unstable cliff here means you should exercise some caution. From here it is a short walk through a cedar-hemlock forest to Clarkes Hollow.

The final and most southerly section is the Walking Trail. This almost 4-km section has a loop roughly two-thirds of the way up. Both parts of the trail in this section are on the east bank of the creek and one travels the valley bottom while the other follows the upland loop.

The trail holds a number of attractions for walkers, including a scenic lookout that offers a magnificent view of the valley. The height of land is the shoreline of Lake Iroquois, the ancient glacial lake that once covered most of this area. Another point of interest is an old trestle bridge that once was used by the Canadian Pacific Railway, but is now abandoned. There are lots of natural areas to walk through, including cedar and mixed bush and a reforestation area. The trail finally ends at the parking lot of the Pickering Day Camp, known as Camp Pidaca.

Short Hills Provincial Park

- **LENGTH:** 9+ km (3+ hours)
- **DEGREE OF DIFFICULTY:** Easy to moderate
- **TYPE OF TRAIL:** Loop • **LOCATION:** Vineland

HOW TO GET THERE:

Take the Queen Elizabeth Highway to exit 57. Drive south on Regional Road 24 approximately 17 km, and turn east onto Highway 20. Drive 6 km to Regional Road 32 (Effingham Road), then north on Effingham Road for about 5.5 km, just past the hydro lines to Roland Road. Turn east onto Roland Road and look

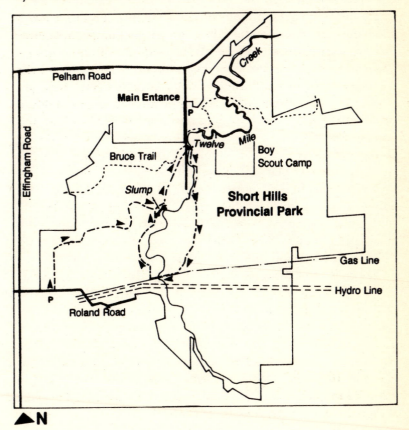

for a parking lot on the north side of the road. There is parking for about six cars.

• • •

Short Hills is an unregulated provincial park located on the Niagara Escarpment not far from Niagara Falls. Because it is unregulated there are no marked trails and no services. No entrance fee is charged. A 19-km network of paths, ski trails and snowmobile trails intersects the 688-ha park so there is no shortage of hiking opportunities. This profusion of unmarked trails tends to be confusing, however, so a topographic map and compass are good hiking companions. A total of 25 km of trails is planned when resources permit.

The park is a gem and an oasis of wilderness on the doorstep of major populations. It will grow more precious as those populations continue to rise. It protects significant Niagara Escarpment features and Carolinian forest, as well as providing a home for wildlife and a retreat for urban dwellers.

As its name implies, the Short Hills landscape is one of undulating hills and valleys. This landscape owes its origin to an ancient valley carved by a pre-glacial river, which probably once connected Lakes Erie and Ontario. Following the retreat of the great ice sheets, glacial deposits filled the valley, shifting the drainage basin to the Niagara River. These glacial deposits were subsequently worn down by erosion, forming the ''short hill'' topography now found in the valley. The glacial deposits also buried the rugged limestone cliffs that are so pronounced on much of the Niagara Escarpment, and they are not prominent here.

The park is in the watershed of Twelve Mile Creek. The creek and its many tributaries snake through the park, tumbling prettily over numerous limestone ledges on the way to Lake Ontario. These, and sweeping panoramic views, make the park an attractive hiking area. The Bruce Trail traverses the park from roughly east to west.

Although the major access point is on the park's north side off the Pelham Road, the trail covered here is accessed from the extreme southwest corner. While it does not visit any waterfalls, it does allow scenic panoramic views and walks through Carolinian forest, and frequently comes into contact with Twelve Mile Creek.

The trail's biggest challenge is crossing the creek where it is about 3 m wide and there is as yet no bridge. This occurs at about the half-way point of the trail.

From the Roland Road parking area, the trail follows a good gravel path for a short way. This path is part of the Palaeozoic Trail, a short, wheelchair-accessible loop that visits Swayze Falls where there is a viewing platform. It is currently the only developed trail in the entire park. At the top of the first hill, the gravel path swings off to the right. Our trail continues straight along a narrow path bordered by sumac and teasels.

Heading directly north, it passes through a reclaimed field surrounded by a pine plantation. Travelling up and down many short hills, the trail passes back into the forest. In the fall, dozens of black walnut trees drop their fruit along the path. After striding across a small stream you will come to a fork in the path. Do not take the fork leading off to the left as it soon leaves the park and enters private property.

The path now leads into a meadow surrounded by oaks. This is a favourite habitat of the wild turkeys that live in the park. The field offers good camouflage with its tall grasses, dogwood, sumac and raspberry bushes, and many bushy wildflowers, such as aster, milkweed and teasel.

Leaving the open area, the path enters the forest again, heading in an easterly direction. Ahead, there are occasional glimpses of rolling hills. A pheasant crows somewhere off to the left. The fruit trees are amazing. In addition to the walnuts there are wild apple and pear trees, the latter bearing honey-sweet fruit. These may be remnants of trees planted by Loyalists and Quakers who were the first settlers. The path travels along the top of a ridge through a lovely Carolinian forest and then drops down the ridge to a stream. Fresh deer tracks are numerous in the soft mud of the stream banks. Close to the stream we can see where a stag has rubbed its antlers against the trunk of a sapling, reducing much of it to fibre.

Across the stream the path bears right and continues through a mixed forest for a short way until it intersects with the stream again. It is wider now, but a couple of small islands make it easy to cross. After winding through the valley bottom the trail splits again and you should follow the narrow path that leads up a steep hill to your right. At the top of the hill, take the fork to your left which leads along the top of the ridge to a T-junction. Turn left here and climb to a meadow from where there are good views behind you of forested hills topped by old white pines.

You are still heading in an easterly direction as you pass through the meadow and arrive at the next T-junction. Turn left and soon you will notice Twelve Mile Creek meandering far below the ridge. Almost immediately you will come to what is known as "The Slump." This is a large area of erosion where the high sandy bank plunges down some 15 m to where the creek bends below.

Just past this, at the bottom of the ridge, the trail intersects with Gilligan Road. Turn right and cross the bridge, then walk up the very high, steep hill. At the top of the hill follow the path that bears right, which climbs another short hill through scrub brush before entering a lovely hardwood forest. The forest floor is littered with multi-coloured leaves on this fall day and ebony spleenwort ferns look rich and green peeping out of their leafy quilt. The path is now heading southeast and you will have been walking about 90 minutes. When the path opens into a field you will see the towers of a hydro corridor dead ahead. Before you reach these the trail swings to the right and follows a buried gas pipeline down a high steep hill to the creek. There is no bridge, however an old, narrow log jammed between the banks is sturdy enough to walk across. It's tricky, and the creek flows swiftly here but is not especially deep. If you lose your balance the worst that can happen is that you will get wet feet.

After climbing the steep bank on the other side of the creek the trail skirts a cultivated field and then swings to the right, heading roughly north again. From here you will walk about 500 m through overgrown fields. Long views of rolling forested hills are dramatic from this high vantage point. On clear days you can catch the odd glimpse of Lake Ontario in the far distance. Over your right shoulder you will see the Brock University Library Tower just clearing the tree tops.

When you come to a split in the trail, take the left fork. You are now on the trail you took into the park, at a point just south of The Slump. From here the parking lot is reached via the same trail that you took on the way in.

Silver Creek and Scotsdale Farm

Bruce Trail

- **LENGTH:** 13 km (5 hours)
- **DEGREE OF DIFFICULTY:** Easy to moderate
- **TYPE OF TRAIL:** Loop • **LOCATION:** Georgetown

HOW TO GET THERE:

Between Georgetown and Acton, Highway 7 makes a curve to the south as it intersects with Trafalgar Road. From Highway 7, follow Trafalgar Road west until it intersects with the 27th Sideroad. Turn right (north). Follow the 27th Sideroad to where it joins the 8th Line. The 27th Sideroad becomes a gravel road and bears

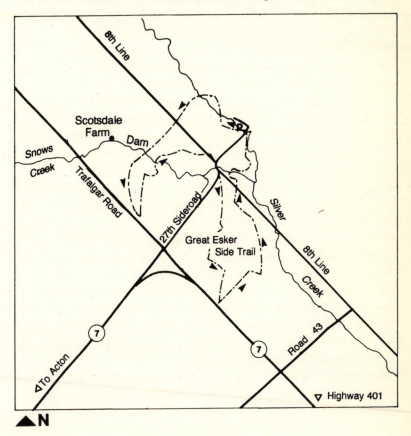

right. Follow this about 1 km until you see a parking area on the east side, just before you get to a bridge. The trail starts across the road.

• • •

A couple of side trails and a stretch of the main Bruce Trail provide an opportunity for a loop hike in a very pretty part of the Niagara Escarpment. Much of the trail follows Silver Creek, a tributary of the Credit River. Part of it is decidedly civilized as it follows the wide gravel paths of the Bennett Heritage Side Trail through Scotsdale Farm. At the other extreme is the trek over the escarpment area south of the 8th Line where you will find yourself literally striding from boulder to boulder on the rocky path. It is a good idea to wear boots if you do this stretch.

The trail starts with a walk along Silver Creek on property belonging to the Credit Valley Conservation Authority. It then enters Scotsdale Farm and joins the main Bruce Trail, crosses the 8th Line and passes through private property. From here it loops again using the Great Esker Side Trail which dips down to Highway 7 and returns to meet the main Bruce Trail just south of the 8th Line. It then skirts the steep edge of the valley carved by Snows Creek and crosses the creek at a very pretty waterfall before returning to the parking area.

To start, cross to the west side of the 27th Sideroad to the Bennett Heritage Side Trail. Look for a blue blaze and a stile at the top of a short, steep bank leading up from the gravel road. When you cross the stile you will see a board with a map of the area. The path leads off to the right along a fence line with a field to your left and the deep, treed ravine of Silver Creek to your right. The land around is undulating and the path leads past banks laden with jewelweed. The creek sings as it flows over its rocky bed.

In about 250 m the trail swings to the left following the line of the creek and then dips into a little valley where there is a pretty pool, its banks festooned with Joe pye-weed, knapweed, chicory and asters. After crossing a short boardwalk and a stile the path enters a field, then skirts the edge of the ravine. After another 250 m the trail enters a wood and dips down to the stream bank where ostrich ferns flourish under big old hardwoods. After paralleling the creek the path turns right and crosses it by a plank bridge. In August, the brilliant scarlet cardinal flower adds a vivid spot of colour on the bank.

The trail now leaves the creek and picks up a wide old cart track, following it through the woods and around the edge of a field until it crosses the creek again. It enters a lovely hardwood forest where moss-covered limestone rocks dot the forest floor. The walking surface is very good. In about 400 m the trail comes to a stile that leads onto the 8th Line, crosses the road and enters Scotsdale Farm.

Scotsdale was donated to the people of Ontario by Stewart and Violet Bennett in 1982. It is managed by the Credit Valley Conservation Authority for the Ontario Heritage Foundation. The path into Scotsdale is used by cars so be alert when walking the 500 m down to the farmsite. This is like a walk down a pleasant country lane. Cows graze in a field to the left and the fence is hung with grapevines. A lovely forest is on your right. The trail follows the lane into the farm, crosses a bridge and winds past the dam which widens Snows Creek into a pool swept by willows. A swan grooms itself on the shore.

The trail goes past farmbuildings and takes a left turn between the barn and the farmhouse lawns, then turns right and passes the house, following the lane between cedar rail fencing. At the end of the fence it turns left into the forest.

The path continues through the forest, and where the trees open up there are views of rolling hills to the right. Just before the path reaches Trafalgar Road, a double blue blaze on a tree shows the trail leading off to the left. Stride over a fence into a little meadow which leads to a junction with the main Bruce Trail. You will now be following a white blaze. Be sure to take the path to the left.

The trail now enters a scrub forest and the path narrows, twisting and turning as it passes through the forest and over numerous boardwalks that cross small streams and swamps. There are many interesting species of fungi, including polypores, the small green parrot mushroom and violet-branched coral.

Passing through the east side of the Scotsdale property, the trail skirts a number of fields, some of which hold cows, and goes in and out of woodlots. It passes through an old orchard where there are numerous deer tracks and, just before it reaches the 8th Line and the 27th Sideroad, the path turns right, crosses a couple of boardwalks and emerges onto the 8th Line.

After crossing the road and following white blazes the path enters a private woodland atop the escarpment. The path through here is not well defined so be sure to follow the blazes, and please respect the owner by not straying off the trail. The forest floor is a boulder field and walking is extremely challenging. After walking about 1 km you will come to a small, mossy crevice and, shortly after that, to the edge of the escarpment. After joining a wider path, the trail meets the start of the Great Esker Side Trail, a 4-km trail that heads off to the right and down a cart track.

Following blue blazes now, the trail descends to cross a swamp that is spanned by two bridges. Continuing southwards it climbs to a rocky outcrop where there are good views, follows the fence line for a while, then goes downhill and crosses a swampy area to emerge at a field. The path goes alongside the edge of the field, makes a sharp left and goes down into a valley. The trail dips into an open field at the bottom of the valley and turns left to start the return trip. After crossing some fields and going through a forest it turns right to climb a ridge (top of the Esker) and turns left. The path descends to a gravel road and shortly re-enters the forest, crosses a streambed and climbs through loose rock to join up with the main Bruce Trail just before it emerges onto the 8th Line. Before crossing the 8th Line, walk up the hill to your right for some fine views of Georgetown in the far distance.

The trail now enters a very pleasant woods and travels along the top of a ravine. Snows Creek, far below, is an impressive sight after heavy rain as it descends the escarpment over a series of falls and rapids. About 10 minutes from the road you will cross the creek by footbridge. This is a good photo stop.

The path continues through the woods, eventually meeting the ravine again where Silver Creek flows down to meet Snows Creek. Watch for an enormous old white pine that is at least 6 m in circumference. Just past this, a snowmobile trail intersects. Be sure to follow the white blazes on the trail that goes off to the left, and not the red blazes of the snowmobile trail, which leads into a swamp. The trail goes over a stile and into a grassy field and you are back at the parking area.

Eastern Ontario

REGIONAL OVERVIEW

FROM THE lowlands of the St. Lawrence River to the forests of the Ottawa and Madawaska valleys, Eastern Ontario is one of the most diverse areas of the province. Hikers can take civilized walks through lovely forests close to the city of Ottawa or follow the rugged **Rideau Trail** across the Frontenac Axis. The hiking opportunities in this part of Ontario are both a surprise and a challenge.

The Rideau Trail is a 300-km trail running between Kingston and Ottawa, roughly paralleling by land the route of the Rideau Waterway. It travels through wild and beautiful areas of the Frontenac Axis, an arm of the Precambrian Shield, as well as over farmland and river valley. The trail is marked by an orange triangle and is accessed from various locations along the route, including short trails in some provincial parks, conservation areas and regional forests. If you are accessing the trail from outside of these public areas a trail guidebook obtainable from the Rideau Trail Association is essential.

Among provincial parks that cater to the hiker is **Charleston Lake**, located on the Frontenac Axis, northeast of Kingston. Here the Westside Trails provide 3-to-4 hours of rugged hiking over quartzite ridges from where there are stunning views of Charleston Lake. Another trail, that goes to the top of Blue Mountain, is primarily a snowmobile trail so it is not in excellent shape for hikers, but can be accessed. The park is reached from Highway 401 East at Lansdowne (Exit 659), then drive north on Highway 3 for 14.5

km to Outlet. More information about the park is available by calling (613) 659-2065.

At **Murphy's Point Provincial Park** the Point Hiking Trail is a loop about 5 km long that travels through mature hardwood forest mostly along the shoreline of Big Rideau Lake. However, the Rideau Trail also passes through the park, which provides additional hiking opportunities. The park is located south of Perth and Smith's Falls on County Road 21. For more information about the park call (613) 267-5060.

Silent Lake near Bancroft offers the 15-km Lakeshore Hiking Trail. This is a rugged trail around the undeveloped shoreline of Silent Lake. There are spectacular lookouts and lots of potential to explore the mineral resources for which the Bancroft area is noted. The park is accessed from Highway 28 south of Bancroft. More information is available from the Bancroft District Office of the Ministry of Natural Resources (613) 332-3940, or from the park at (613) 339-2807.

The trails at **Presqu'ile Provincial Park** on Lake Ontario are mainly for birdwatchers and wetland enthusiasts. At least 310 species of birds have been spotted within the park's boundaries. Trails are through forested lands and along the beach, as well as into the wetland via a boardwalk. The park is reached from Highway 401 at Brighton (Exit 509), then travel south on Highway 30 until you see the park signs. For more information from the park call (416) 475-2204.

Conservation areas in Eastern Ontario meet a good many hiking needs with a great variety of trails. The **Vanderwater Conservation Area** north of Belleville has six trails totalling 23 km. Included are walks through mature cedar forests as well as groves of hardwood and coniferous trees. A high ridge runs through the property from where there are good views to the west. Trails are accessed from Highway 37, north of Belleville, 3 km west of Thomasburg. More information from the Vanderwater Conservation Authority is available by calling (613) 968-3434.

The **Goodrich-Loomis Conservation Area** has more than 15 km of trails in 208 ha of woodlands located in hilly country just north of Lake Ontario. From Highway 401, (Exit 509) go north on Highway 30. Look for the Conservation Area sign in the village of Orland, then go west on a back road for about 2 km. For more information from the Lower Trent Region Conservation Authority call (613) 394-4829.

There are 40 km of trails in the **Northumberland County Forest** and the neighbouring **Peter's Woods Nature Reserve**. The trails are groomed for cross-country skiing in winter, but in summer are open to hikers, mountain bikers and equestrians. The trails can be looped for long hikes. In the Peter's Woods Nature Reserve are remnants of the magnificent hardwood forests that once covered much of southern Ontario, as well as several large white pines. The Northumberland County Forest is located on Highway 45, 14 km north of Cobourg. From the hamlet of Baltimore, continue north to Beagle Club Road and turn left, then watch for the parking lot. More information is available from the Ministry of Natural Resources, Napanee District Office, by calling (613) 354-2173.

Closer to Ottawa, the 7,000-ha **Marlborough Forest** has endless opportunities for hiking, although there are as yet only short marked trails. However, the area is intersected by several fire roads, and the Rideau Trail skirts the forest. It is a jewel of a place close to major populations with a variety of wetlands, mixed woods, swamps, marshes and fens. It is also the home of a number of rare plants, such as the walking fern and several species of orchids. A map and compass is essential if you intend to get off the beaten track. From Ottawa, take Highway 16 south to Roger Stevens Drive. Turn west and drive through North Gower. Ten km from here Roger Stevens Drive passes through the centre of the forest. For more information contact the Regional Municipality of Ottawa-Carleton at (613) 560-2053.

East of Ottawa, at Fitzroy Harbour on the Ottawa River, the **Morris Island Conservation Area** has some pretty trails on a string of islands in the river. The 47-ha site has forested woodlands and wetlands to explore and spectacular views of the Ottawa River. Obtain more information from the Mississippi Valley Conservation Authority at (613) 259-2421 or 1-800-267-1659.

In the gorgeous Madawaska Highlands, the **Madawaska River Provincial Park** is a favourite destination of whitewater canoeists. But so much beauty should be shared, so a new hiking trail is being developed on Mount Jamieson on the north side of the river. It is accessed from an unbelievably rugged bush road that runs between Palmer Rapids and Griffith. It is hard to find, so phone the Ministry of Natural Resources, Pembroke District Office at (613) 732-3661 for directions.

Finally, the **Pakkotinna Recreational Trail** is a 40-km all-purpose trail running roughly north-south between Highway 62, 24 km west of Pembroke, and Golden Lake. This is a trail on Crown lands that follows old logging roads. It was developed mainly as a snowmobile trail but provides opportunities for hikers to walk some quiet bush roads. Check with the Ministry of Natural Resources Pembroke District Office before setting out to ascertain trail conditions. Access from the north end is from a parking lot west of the town of Alice on Highway 62. From the south there is a parking lot on Highway 60, about 8 km west of Golden Lake.

Abes and Essens Trail

Bon Echo Provincial Park

- **LENGTH**: 4, 9 and 17 km (90 minutes to 7+ hours)
- **DEGREE OF DIFFICULTY**: Easy to challenging
- **TYPE OF TRAIL**: Three loops • **LOCATION**: Cloyne

HOW TO GET THERE:

Follow Highway 41, north from Napanee to the park, 10 km north of Cloyne. Turn right into the park entrance and drive to the gate house, where you must stop and register. Just past the gate house make a left turn onto the Joeperry Lake Road which runs westward underneath Highway 41. There is a parking lot on the south side just east of Hardwood Hill Campground. The trail

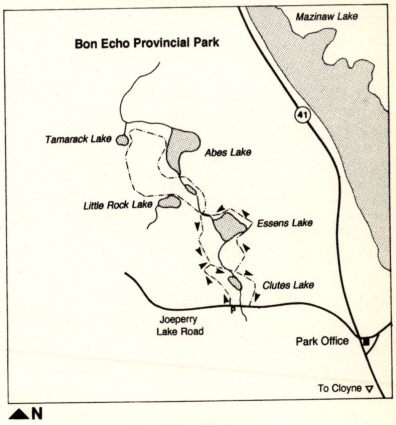

starts across the road and heads north. The provincial park charges a day-use fee and normally closes after Labour Day.

• • •

This beautiful 6,644-ha area of forests and lakes located on the Frontenac Axis of the Canadian Shield is a favourite of hikers. The Abes and Essens Trail has three loops and the hiker can choose to do one, two or all three. Tackling all three in one day, however, is for the adventurous and very fit and doesn't leave much time to enjoy the park's wilderness flavour. There are campsites on the trail and if you want to hike the whole thing, this may be a good time to try an overnight hike. Book your campsite well in advance.

For a day hike, the trail around Essens and Clutes lakes is recommended. It will take about 4 hours of steady walking but is longer with breaks for lunch and to enjoy the scenery.

Bon Echo is an area of many lakes, the largest and most prominent being Mazinaw Lake, dominated by the formidable Mazinaw Rock. This was billed as the "Canadian Gibraltar" in early travel brochures. The area has a fascinating history of aboriginal use and legends, of logging and pioneer settlement. The area around Mazinaw Lake was bought in 1889 by Dr. Weston A. Price for a luxury inn and resort. He named the resort Bon Echo for the reflected sound effects produced by The Rock.

By the turn of the century the resort was in the hands of Flora MacDonald Denison, a Toronto businesswoman, journalist, and women's rights advocate. Mrs. Denison transformed the resort into a cultural centre, with American poet Walt Whitman as its particular cultural focus. A huge Whitman memorial is carved into the cliff face.

The cultural theme of the place continued when Merrill Denison, writer and son of Flora, assumed control of the resort. He persuaded several members of the Group of Seven to paint in the area and also to illustrate the resort's brochures and other publicity material.

The Group of Seven were not the first artists to record their impressions of the area. Generations ago, aboriginal shamans painted pictures on the huge cliff face as a beautiful and mysterious tribute. Today, the park continues the area's cultural tradition by naming a writer-in-residence.

The Abes and Essens Hiking Trail takes you away from Mazinaw Lake and the cliff, and into the remote outer reaches of the park to the northwest. The park lies on the Frontenac Arm of the Canadian Shield and the scenery is rugged, wild and beautiful. The trail is a lonely one, and it gets lonelier the farther you travel. This area is home to black bear, moose, white-tailed deer, timber wolf, beaver and other northern creatures, as well as wildlife normally found in southern Ontario, such as the turkey vulture and the five-lined skink, a small lizard.

The first loop is the Clutes Lake Loop, an easy walk around the tiny lake. The loops become more adventurous the farther you go, and they can be distinguished by small red, yellow or orange disks.

The Clutes Lake Loop is popular and the trail is easy to follow as it is well travelled and topped with woodchips. If you are hiking this trail in August, look for the brilliant scarlet cardinal flower which grows in marshy ground near the footbridge over the creek that flows into Clutes Lake at the head of the first trail.

The brilliance of the cardinal flower is almost eclipsed by the sheer variety of fungi on the trail. All shapes, sizes and colours, from the orange- and white-dotted fly agaric that we all know are homes for the little folk, to the pristine white parasol called the destroying angel. There are oyster mushrooms and angel wings, and a multitude of gorgeous pinks, mauves, scarlets and yellows that shine in the dark earth beneath the trees.

The head of the first loop is just to the west of the little footbridge that spans the stream draining Essens Lake. To get to the second (Essens Lake) trail, it is a good idea to walk up the east side of the stream, so cross the bridge and walk north beside some enormous boulders that were left here by the last ice age. If you are ready for a rest, climb up and sit on the rocks overlooking the bridge. The view looks almost too contrived, as though it had been professionally landscaped.

The route up the east side is popular with hikers, heading for remote campsites, who usually return by the same route. This means the path is well worn and easily followed.

From the large boulders, follow the yellow signs as the path climbs upwards and passes the first campsite on the trail. This area was logged in the last century for its white pines so the forest is young. Blackened stumps here and there tell the story of forest fires that swept the area. Today, a young pine, poplar, birch and maple forest nurtures the area's wildlife.

At the second campsite, on high boulders overlooking an inlet, there are lovely views down the lake, where white pines crowd the shoreline. The trail continues tracing the eastern shoreline of the lake, climbing steeply in some places for panoramic views. It then descends very sharply to a swampy area close to the lake head. The walking is rough here and quite wet but there are stepping stones leading to a boardwalk.

A long hill leads up from the lake and the open tree canopy allows the sunshine in to dapple the ferns and gleam on the red fruit of the bunchberry. At the head of the lake is a beaver dam. The trail continues northwards for about 100 m where it meets up with the start of the Abes Trail. The Essens Trail turns left and crosses some boulders to the other side of a little creek. It climbs a short, steep hill and soon intersects with the return loop of the Abes Trail. From here it loops southwards, travelling through a very much drier ecosystem than that on the east side of the lake. There are fewer fungi and lots of evidence of past forest fires.

The trail continues southward, offering views of the lake before heading into the forest. It passes a swampy area and arrives at the head of the Clutes Lake Loop. You have a choice here of returning to the parking lot down the west side of Clutes Lake, or recrossing the footbridge and returning down the east side for a complete loop.

The third trail, which leads the hiker past Abes and Tamarack lakes, is a wilderness trail that offers real adventure. It is very rugged and not often used so you will need to watch carefully for orange-coloured trail markers on the trees. This trail is not for the novice and those hiking it should be ready for primitive conditions. It crosses many low lying areas and the hiker should be prepared for wet feet. Although there are small bridges in some places, in others beavers have moved in and caused the trail to be washed out.

On this third loop look for numerous trees at the side of the trail that are scarred by the long, sharp claws of black bears. Biologists believe the black bear scratches trees to mark its territory.

On this trail you may also see evidence of moose as droppings are often found close to the trail.

Foley Mountain Trails

Rideau Trail System

- **LENGTH**: 5 km (2 hours) • **DEGREE OF DIFFICULTY**: Easy
- **TYPE OF TRAIL**: Loop • **LOCATION**: Westport

HOW TO GET THERE:

From Westport, cross the easternmost of the village's two bridges that span Upper Rideau Lake and follow Regional Road 10 to the top of the mountain. Turn left into Foley Mountain Conservation Area. Follow the conservation area road until you see a parking lot sign on your right.

• • •

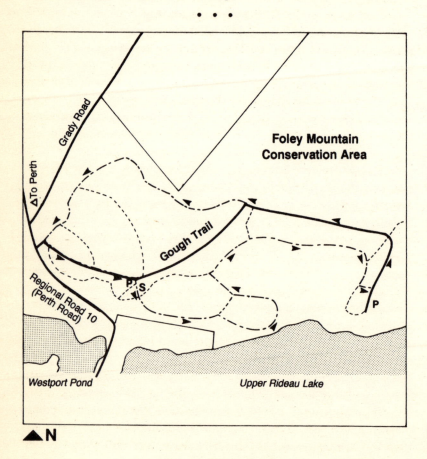

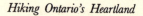

There are numerous trails in the 308-ha Foley Mountain Conservation Area and many are used by tourists looking for quick photo opportunities. Lookouts over Upper Rideau Lake are easily reached by short trails from the parking lot and they offer outstanding views over this historic waterway. Hikers who want a longer walk can pick up a conservation area trail map and plan a variety of loop hikes around the park. There is also the opportunity to experience some 5 km of the famous Rideau Trail as it traverses the highest elevation of the entire trail (207 m above sea level). Paths are marked by orange triangles for the Rideau Trail, blue for the Foley Mountain Conservation Area side trails.

Westport lies on the eastern rim of the Frontenac Axis, an arm of the Canadian Shield that dips southwards through the middle of eastern Ontario, bringing a touch of "up north" to this area. Foley Mountain is a rugged escarpment that towers over Upper Rideau Lake, offering opportunities for some challenging hiking, as well as for viewing landscapes normally found much farther north. There is no charge for using the trails, or the picnic area and lovely swimming beach. The conservation area is operated by the Rideau Valley Conservation Authority which manages and protects 4,095 km² of the Rideau Valley watershed.

The village of Westport was so named because of its location at the western end of Upper Rideau Lake. At one time it was on the Kingston-to-Ottawa steamer route. Surveyed in 1803, it was settled by pioneer farmers before becoming a centre of industry with feed and saw mills, a woolen mill, brickyard, tannery and other industries. Today, capitalizing on its lovely scenery, Westport concentrates on tourism, serving the many boaters on the Rideau Waterway and the many visitors who come by road.

Foley Mountain is a good area to hike if you are an inexperienced hiker as it offers a lot of the rewards of remote hiking without some of the drawbacks. It is an excellent area to introduce youngsters to the attractions of hiking.

Before starting the trail from the Foley Mountain Conservation Area parking lot, you may wish to double back to take a quick look at Spy Rock a few metres to the east. There is a stupendous view of Westport and the Westport Pond. Retrace your steps back to the parking lot and begin your hike on the trail named Scenic

Ridge Trail. Follow this trail as it winds through the woods and over rocky outcroppings for about 500 m to reach the first scenic lookout. This offers a view over Upper Rideau Lake and the eastern end of the village, beyond which flat farmland stretches away to the east.

Continue on over huge pink whaleback-shaped granite outcroppings and through grassy areas where yellow coreopsis glows in the sunshine. If you listen carefully you may hear the eastern peewee calling through the woods, or catch a glimpse of a crested flycatcher.

When you come to a Parking Lot sign, keep to the right and follow the trail down through the woods where glimpses of the lake can be seen between the trees. At the next Y-junction, there is a sign that points to Rockslide Lookout. The path leads down a torturous trail where you will need to hang on to the trees to keep from slipping. The path culminates at a huge rockslide, or scree, that tumbles down the escarpment. You will need to climb back up the slope to regain the main trail.

Continuing along the top of the ridge, the trail heads away from the lake. Some enormous boulders lie on the left of the path, which then snakes to the right and crosses the top of the rockslide. A little farther along the path turns towards the lake again and there is another scenic lookout. Clumps of blueberry bushes grow in sparse soil around the rocks. In season, look for the helleborine orchid in the woods around here.

When you leave the scenic lookout, take the path that leads away from the lake, not the path that goes straight ahead and leads nowhere. On the way uphill, look for a huge old tree trunk on your right. When you come to the granite outcrops follow the blue markers to your right. There are lots of gorgeous fungi in the woods around here—all colours, shapes and sizes, ranging from the pretty fly agaric that you have seen in children's picture books, to the fluffy white bear's head coral fungus. There are also orchids in spring.

The trail crosses a swamp by means of a boardwalk and stepping stones and continues through pine woods just to the left of a little swamp. After passing the swamp you will round a bend and see blue and orange markers on a tree. This is a bit confusing. Continue straight ahead, following the orange trail signs into a hardwood forest. A little way along there is another blue trail marker leading off to the right. This goes down to the Foley Mountain Conservation Area Interpretive Centre. Our trail continues following the orange markers, goes downhill, crosses a small bridge over a pretty little stream and shortly emerges onto a gravel road, named Gough Trail. The Rideau Trail, with its orange markers, crosses the road and disappears into the woods on its long haul to Ottawa.

You will now have been walking about 80 minutes. If the weather is warm, you may want to break the walk here by turning right and walking down to the beach for a swim. Otherwise, to continue the trail, turn left and walk up the gravel road. The walking now is easy. The gravel road is lined with wildflowers, including the ubiquitous purple loosestrife, that beautiful but deadly destroyer of our wetlands. Also here are jewelweed, purple raspberry, viper's bugloss and pearly everlasting, not to mention wild grapes and sweet-smelling milkweed.

If you want to cut your hike short at this point you can follow the gravel road about 1 km to the parking lot.

For a longer, more interesting walk, follow the road until you come to a fork where you will see a sign that says "Private" on a road branching off to the right. Pass this and look for a blue marker leading into the bush on your right, following it into a reclaimed meadow. The path goes into a mixed forest and takes a turn to the right along a fence line.

After leaving the fence, look for an enormous maple that is awe inspiring. It must be a couple of hundred years old, is about 5 m in diameter, and bears correspondingly large fungi on its trunk. A little farther along there is also an enormous white pine. The path continues into a young pine plantation and runs close to a large, ancient oak.

A side trail along here leads to a beaver pond, or you can continue on, crossing a small footbridge and following blue trail markers. When you come to an area where a number of trails converge and there is a "No. 10" marked on a tree, bear right. This will lead you back to the gravel road again, close to the entrance to the conservation area. Turn left onto the gravel road and you are about 5 minutes from your car.

Eastern Ontario

Trails of Frontenac Provincial Park

- **LENGTH:** 1 to 170+ km (1 hour to several days)
- **DEGREE OF DIFFICULTY:** Varied. Mostly challenging
- **TYPE OF TRAIL:** Loop and linear • **LOCATION:** Sydenham

HOW TO GET THERE:

Take Highway 38 north of Kingston to Harrowsmith. Turn east on County Road 5 to Sydenham, then drive north on County Road 19 for about 10 km. Watch for the Frontenac Provincial Park signs on the east side of the road, then turn onto Frontenac Park Road and follow the signs to the park entrance.

• • •

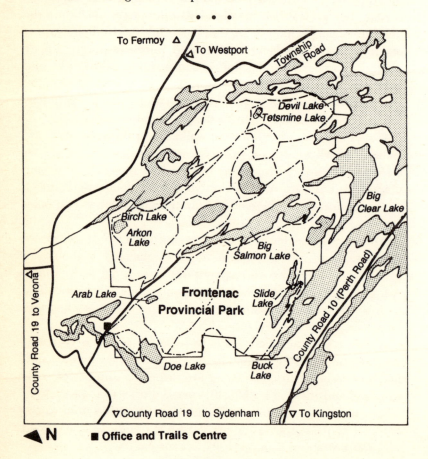

The sight of a couple of startled fawns scampering across the road as you drive up to the park entrance is a fitting introduction to Frontenac Provincial Park. It tells you that if you are looking to view wildlife in its natural habitat you have come to the right place.

It is easy to understand why this park attracts wilderness seekers from across the world. It is a hiker's paradise, with more than 170 km of wilderness and semi-wilderness trails for both day hikers and extended-stay backpackers. It is also one of the few parks in the Ontario provincial parks system that caters almost exclusively to the backcountry enthusiast—both hiker and canoeist. There are no drive-in campsites.

The park sprawls across almost 70 km² of northern-Ontario-style landscape on the Frontenac Axis, a southern extension of the Precambrian Shield. It brings to this part of southern Ontario much of the landscape characteristics associated with the Shield— the granite outcroppings, the varied forest cover and the animals, such as otter, wolf, bobcat and the occasional moose, as well as some 400 head of deer. Park users also claim to have seen the rare and elusive eastern cougar in the north end of the park.

The park's location also attracts creatures more common to southern climes. One is the black rat snake, Canada's only constrictor, which can grow as large as four metres. It is rarely seen, harmless to humans and is on the endangered species list, as is the five-lined skink, Ontario's only lizard, which also is found in the park.

Rare plants grow here too. One is the puttyroot, a member of the orchid family, which reportedly was last seen in Ontario in an Ottawa cemetery, disappearing in the 1930s. It was discovered growing in the park only recently. There is also a community of rare ferns growing just north of Black Lake, one of only two occurrences in Canada. The other location is east of Montreal. One of the park's major claims to fame is a black-fly season that is only two weeks long. Unlike areas farther north, these pesky critters are normally gone from Frontenac by about the third week of May.

The park landscape is rugged and beautiful, and typically Shield country with its representative granite cliffs, ridges, rocky outcroppings and numerous lakes, beaver ponds, swamps and bogs.

Eleven long-distance trails put most of the park literally at the feet of the hiker. You can choose to backpack in and spend a weekend or several days exploring Frontenac. Or, amazingly, the park is less than an hour's drive from the city of Kingston so you can hike during the day and have all the comfort a city hotel room can offer overnight, if that's your style.

Trails are accessible from three drive-in areas near the park entrance, which is located at the extreme southwestern end of the park. Alternatively there are a couple of unofficial entrances. One is at the northwest edge of the park, entering from an unnamed Township Road that curves southwards from the village of Salem. The other follows part of the Rideau Trail from Perth County Road 10 to the Slide Lake Loop on the southeastern end of the park. The park has two Slide Lake Loops. One is a short version that loops around Slide Lake itself, while a longer loop continues north and west to join up with the Cedar Lake Loop. The Slide Lake Short Loop is covered elsewhere in this book.

A visit to the park usually starts with a 15-20 minute audio-visual presentation given by staff to orientate visitors to park features and facilities. Hikers are given an an opportunity to ask questions and plan their routes on a huge map of the park. Frontenac staff also teach a wilderness skills training program, which is offered year-round.

The orientation includes an overview of the park's history, and staff explain that despite its wilderness flavour the park area has been a focus for homesteaders, logging and mining over the last 100 years. Evidence of these activities abound in the park. Old roads that once were transportation routes to mica mines and pioneer farmsteads now serve as trails for the hiker.

Much of the area in the southern part of the park was logged in the late 1800s for its huge white pine timbers. Shortly afterwards there was a massive fire, then in the early 1900s it was logged for hemlock, followed by another fire. All of this has left some areas so eroded that they present an extremely rugged face; bare rock and lakes surrounded by scrubby trees combine for a starkly beautiful landscape.

A look at the park map reveals a honeycomb of trails covering the entire park area. Many of these visit abandoned mica mines, heronries, scenic ridges and pretty lakes. Hikers can just about always find a deserted beach for a swim.

Trails in the southern portion of the park, close to the trails centre, include the Arab Lake Gorge Trail, an easy 40-minute introduction to the park. The trail follows a lengthy boardwalk, passing between the sheer rock walls of the Gorge, one of the park's oldest geological faults. The next shortest walk is the 3-km Doe Lake Loop which leads the hiker past several beaver ponds and a deserted trapper's shack, an osprey nest and a scenic viewpoint overlooking Doe Lake.

The Kingston-to-Ottawa Rideau Trail also traverses the rugged southern portion of the park for 20 km, entering at the trails centre and ending at Perth County Road 10. On its way it climbs Flagpole Hill, an exposed dome-shaped hill topped by a large dead tree that looks like a flagpole. The hill is the highest point in the park and the views from it are remarkable. Longer trails in the southern third of the park include the 13-km Arkon Lake Loop, a wide circle loop that leads the hiker past remains of turn-of-the-century homesteads and along pioneer roadbeds, as well as beaver ponds and heronries.

The Frontenac Park Road leads to the southwestern tip of Big Salmon Lake and there is a worthwhile 19-km hike around the lake that traverses scenic ridges and brings the hiker into contact with old fishing and hunting cabins and pioneer farmsteads. The trail leads through hardwood forests that offer wonderful fall colour tours.

Trails in the northern portion of the park are dominated by the far-reaching arms of Devil Lake, which probe into the park from the main body of the lake to the east. Rolling hills and valleys carpeted with rich hardwood forests are a surprising contrast to the open, rocky ridges of the south. There's history here in the form of many old mica mines. The 14-km Tetsmine Lake Loop leads the hiker past the old Tett Mine, which was, for a time, the largest producer of mica in Ontario. A large part of the trail follows old road beds.

History, rugged beauty, wilderness trails both long and short— Frontenac has what it takes to keep hikers happy for many an hour.

Slide Lake Loop

Rideau Trail—Frontenac Provincial Park

- **LENGTH:** 15 km (6 hours)
- **DEGREE OF DIFFICULTY:** Challenging
- **TYPE OF TRAIL:** Loop • **LOCATION:** Sydenham

HOW TO GET THERE:

This loop of the Rideau Trail is on the east side of Frontenac Provincial Park. (Note: on the provincial park trail map this trail is shown as the Slide Lake Short Loop.) From Kingston take County Road 10 (Perth Road) North. Drive for about 30 minutes until you pass Raymond's Corners, then look for a nursing home on your right. A little farther on you will see a gravel parking lot

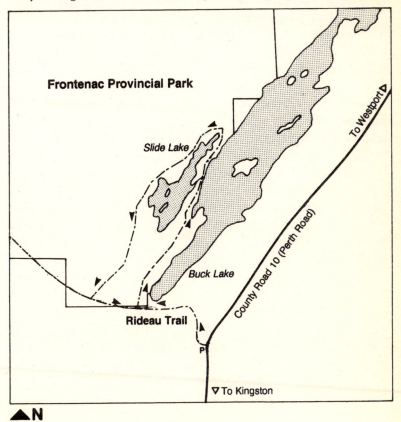

on the west side of the road. Park here and walk down the old abandoned Perth Road to access the trail.

• • •

This is one of the few loops on the Rideau Trail and it is rugged but well worth the effort. You'll take a walk around a small, beautiful lake, climbing to headlands that offer stunning views. You'll experience a number of wetlands and swamps, and the wildlife associated with these, and have lots of opportunities for wildlife viewing.

The loop must be accessed from the main Rideau Trail and some parts of the trail just off the highway are daunting. But press on, good things await you. The main trail is delineated by an orange triangular marker, while the side trail which takes you around Slide Lake has a blue marker. Be sure to follow these markers at all times because the trail around Slide Lake is not well travelled so there is no well-defined path, particularly around the west side.

From the parking lot, look for the orange marker at the south end of the lot. This will lead you to the old highway which is on a lower level than the present one. When you reach this, turn right and follow it for about 300 m until you see the orange sign pointing into the bush on your left. The path leads away from the road and through thick bush until you climb to higher ground. In a few minutes you will arrive at a huge rockface on the other side of a wide swamp where brilliant green duckweed forms a thick mat on the surface. The swamp is crossed via some logs. On the other side, a narrow path travels underneath the rockface, using a number of old logs to negotiate various wet spots. The first of many garter snakes slithers across the path and disappears beneath the duckweed. The place seems threatening and at this point you will probably want to turn back, but keep on, the obstacles are almost out of the way.

Eventually, after squeezing around the side of the rockface, you will climb it and once on higher ground the landscape appears much less intimidating. From this high ground you will have a view of Buck Lake, a quite large body of water which you will see close up once you start walking the Slide Lake Loop.

The trail continues through the woods in an up-and-down

fashion until you come to a tree that has both a red and blue arrow on it, and the word "View." If you follow the signs to the right and up to the top of the rocks there is an interesting view of Buck Lake and the rolling forested hills. No need to retrace your steps, the trail continues from here and descends into a deep gorge, climbs out of it and enters, of all things, a farmer's field where there are cows. A map of the Slide Lake Loop is in the field, courtesy of Frontenac Provincial Park, in which the Slide Lake Loop is located. The trail, however, is maintained by the Rideau Trail Association. The map indicates that you have now reached South Side Junction.

To access the Slide Lake Loop trail, follow the blue markers across the field and along the right hand side of a beaver pond where there is a heronry. The herons appear quite miffed at the appearance of hikers and rise from their nests squawking. A couple of osprey circle overhead.

After about 300 m the trail goes into the woods and then down into a gully where you will negotiate a beaver dam using old logs. This is followed by a climb up a cliff where, at the top, dozens of partridge rise in a flurry of feathers. Around here, also, there are some curious scratches on the trunk of a birch tree that look as though they may have been made by a bear.

The path continues through the woods under a fairly open canopy, which allows sunlight to filter through onto large patches of black-eyed Susans. The path emerges into a regenerating meadow and then enters a pleasant hardwood bush. Soon, glimpses of Buck Lake appear to the right. In a meadow there is a remote campsite and privy.

Leaving the meadow, the path enters a pine forest that is changing into a maple bush. There are lots of interesting fungi in here, as well as helleborine orchid and Solomon's seal. A lovely, purple-fringed orchis was a special find.

The path veers left and brings you to the shore of Buck Lake. Soon you are walking along a high, narrow ridge with Buck Lake to the east and Slide Lake to the west. Buck Lake is a large, developed lake, however Slide Lake is small, seldom visited and lovely. Rocky headlands, topped with white pines, plunge steeply into the water and there are a number of islands, thickly forested with white pine. A couple of immature loons fish lazily for lunch.

The trail passes a tiny inlet of Slide Lake where starkly white water-lilies turn yellow-centred faces to the sun. It then descends to a minute beach on Buck Lake where a pretty waterfall spills the waters of Slide Lake some 16 m into Buck Lake. Brilliant scarlet cardinal flowers at the edge of the waterfall make it look almost too perfect. The path goes up by the waterfall, then crosses the stream by a small footbridge. From here, the trail passes through a swamp and climbs a steep hill where there are marvelous views of Buck Lake. After going down an incline, you will emerge onto a very steep cliff. The path then turns away from Buck Lake and comes out above the head of Slide Lake. After going down a cliff, the path crosses a footbridge where there are more cardinal flowers and you can see Slide Lake stretching in a long line to the south. In a minute you will come to the North Side Junction trail map. You will now have been on the trail 2 hours, 40 minutes. The map shows a trail leading off to the right, to a campsite on Big Salmon Lake, 5 km north.

If you lunch here, watch for poison ivy on the rocks. From here on you will encounter the plant frequently on rocky outcroppings above Slide Lake.

There are better lunch stops a little farther on where the trail passes over huge whale-backed rocks overlooking the west side of the lake. The walk here is a delight, though rugged. The lake stretches below in a basin and the views are outstanding. From some vantage points you can see just about all of the lake and its islands. Trail club members have erected cairns on a number of rocks that are useful guides. Look for deer because the amount of scat indicates the animals visit here frequently. The path travels in and out of the woods, and across a number of beaver dams, then up and over more rocky outcrops. It makes a sharp descent to cross a plank bridge over a reach of the lake, then is faced by a solid mass of rock that appears daunting. It is best negotiated by climbing up about halfway, then veering to the right, climbing some more, and finally climbing to the left to reach the top.

The path travels on top of the cliff a short way, then goes down to the lake where you can wet your feet if you want. Blue flags grow near the shore. After climbing again it continues along the tops of huge, smooth rocks, then descends away from the lake to cross a beaver dam. The trail then enters a wood and, on leaving it, climbs another ridge and runs alongside a swamp. From here it follows a series of switchbacks over ridges, coming alongside another swamp where there are many dead trees. After climbing a rock pile the trail enters the woods and brings you to the sign for the West Slide Junction.

Turn left and follow both blue and orange markers for 1.5 km, passing through the woods and crossing a swamp, then turning left underneath a huge rockface. The trail opens into a couple of open meadows and crosses them to reach West Slide Junction again. Finish the trail by retracing your original path back to the Perth Road, 2.7 km from here.

Gould Lake Conservation Area

Rideau Trail System

- **LENGTH:** 3 to 15+ km (1 hour to 5+ hours)
- **DEGREE OF DIFFICULTY:** Easy to challenging
- **TYPE OF TRAIL:** Loop • **LOCATION:** Sydenham

HOW TO GET THERE:

Gould Lake Conservation Area is located 5 km north of Sydenham, off the 7th Concession on Gould Lake Road. Follow Conservation Area signs north from County Road 19, in Sydenham. There is a day-use fee paid on an honour basis.

• • •

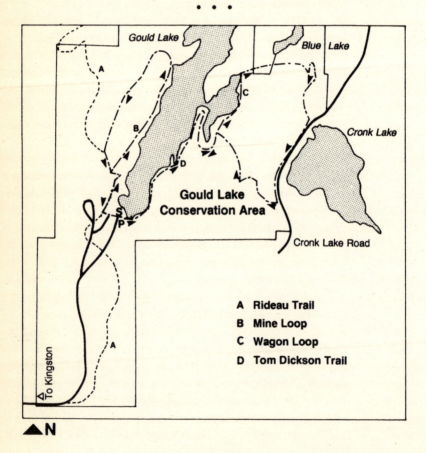

A Rideau Trail
B Mine Loop
C Wagon Loop
D Tom Dickson Trail

The trails in Gould Lake Conservation Area, operated by the Cataraqui Conservation Authority, offer opportunities for both the novice and seasoned hiker to experience the rugged Rideau Trail system. Trails vary from a quick evening hike to one that can be stretched into a day with lunch and a swim in summer. The main Rideau Trail traverses the eastern rim of the conservation area and the trail association maintains a network of loop trails throughout the 589-ha wilderness area.

The park is located on the rugged Frontenac Axis, an arm of the Precambrian Shield that plunges southward here, far from its usual more northerly location. This unique geological system provides an opportunity for southeastern Ontario residents and visitors to experience terrain, wildlife and plantlife normally associated with landscapes of northern Ontario. The area is home to white-tailed deer, and the rare and endangered black rat snake, a huge amphibian growing some two metres or more long. It is not dangerous to humans. Another rare amphibian found here is the five-lined skink, and there is a bountiful crop of wildflowers and unusual fungi. The lakes are clear and cold and lovely for swimming, fishing and canoeing. An abundance of hardwoods make fall trails colourful and beautiful.

Trails are accessed from a parking lot at the entrance to the Gould Lake Conservation Area close to an old barn that serves as an interpretive centre. From here you can make your choice of several trails, such as the short Mine Loop on the west shore of Gould Lake, which visits old mica mines and travels part of the main Rideau Trail. Or you can take the Tom Dickson Trail, which traverses the eastern shore of the lake, linking up with several other loops to provide limitless opportunities for hikes.

To follow the Mine Loop, cross the large grassy area past the barn and take the very noticeable path that runs up a steep incline. An excellent swimming beach is on your right. You will be following blue markers until you get to the mine, when the path will be joined by the orange isosceles triangles of the Rideau Trail. The path rises steeply until it is high over the lake, then descends the other side almost immediately. At the bottom of the slope the path leads over the Marion Webb Boardwalk, a long walkway erected in 1987 by the Rideau Trail Association. The boardwalk spans a large wetland and halfway across there is a seat so that you can comfortably survey the scene.

The trail continues through cedar bush and into a reclaimed field area, brushing through unusually high junipers. Open areas here are garden-like and glistening with pretty mauve knapweed and sunny coreopsis. The rabbits here must be breeding like, well, rabbits. They are all over the place.

The trail enters a hardwood forest, winds down to the lake and travels up and down numerous ridges. Some of the climbs up and down these ridges are tricky and you will need to choose your footing carefully in order not to slide. As you walk over the rocky outcrops, notice the mica glistening as the sun hits the rocks. Pioneer farmers, lured to this part of Ontario by promises of rich, arable land, often supplemented their incomes by mining when the lands proved largely unsuitable for agriculture.

The trail drops down a steep incline to a swamp where there is a short boardwalk. A little farther on there is a junction of trails and you can, if you wish, take a spur trail to the right which leads to a lookout. You will need to return the same way.

The mine loop continues straight on and travels through a pleasant, open, grassy area with lots of wildflowers. The trail takes a sharp turn to the west and climbs a short hill to get to the mine, a fenced-off excavation in the rock, about 2 m wide by 6 m long and about 3 m deep. Long unused, nature has taken over and the mine is now filled with water. Tiny ferns and mosses grow in crevices. Shards of mica lay all around and litter the return path.

To return to base, follow the fence line to the left and down the old mine road. The walking along here is pleasant and easy. In about 500 m you will come to another abandoned mine and if you look closely you can see veins of mica in the rockface. Just past this excavation there is a swamp where, in August, you can see the brilliant red cardinal flower.

Hiking Ontario's Heartland

The trail next enters a reclaimed meadow and the path narrows considerably, winding between huge junipers and sumacs. It emerges, once again, at the Marion Webb Boardwalk. You then have a choice of returning to the parking area by retracing your steps up the high hill, or bearing right and following the old mine road around the edge of the rockface. Following the old mine road, you will see a swamp to the right. Continue following the old road to the top of the hill to where there are some fenced-off caves to your right. Follow the path until it emerges at the grassy picnic area close to the parking lot for a total walk of about 4 km.

The Tom Dickson Trail, which travels the east side of the lake, is part of a loop system. It was named as a tribute to a young student employee of the Cataraqui Conservation Authority who drowned in the lake when the trail was being built in the summer of 1971. This trail also starts from the parking lot but goes off to the right along the south end of Gould Lake. After climbing a steep hill, where there are long views of the lake, it descends to just above the lake level and follows the line of the lake until it drops to a long sandy beach.

The trail then heads east following the line of a small peninsula and in about 200 m crosses a log bridge over a creek to a site known

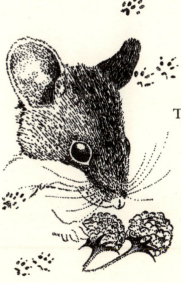

as Porky Junction, where it meets Wagon Trail. Wagon Trail heads east to the Cronk Lake Road, following an old wagon trail built about 1890 to carry mica out from the numerous mines in the area. The Tom Dickson Trail continues northward around a narrow bay of the lake and climbs steeply to the top of a cliff. The lake can be seen through the trees. The climb down is just as steep and descends almost to the lake. In about 500 m the Tom Dickson Trail ends and you have a choice of routes.

You can turn left and follow the Mica Trail, a rugged loop trail of almost 4 km, before returning to the parking lot the way you came in via the Tom Dickson Trail. Alternatively, you can swing eastwards on the East Trail about 1 km, emerge onto Cronk Lake Road, then follow Cronk Lake Road south about 1 km to pick up the Wagon Trail leading back to the Tom Dickson Trail and eventually to the parking lot. This is a total of approximately 8 km, excluding the Mica Trail.

Picturesque Katherine Cove in Lake Superior Provincial Park is one access point for the park's 63 km Coastal Trail, which also forms a section of the 500 km Voyageur Trail. The Voyageur traces the shoreline of most of Ontario's share of this great lake, and a major portion runs through magnificent Lake Superior Provincial Park, north of Sault Ste. Marie. The Coastal Trail takes up to 7 days to complete, although access points such as this one at Katherine Cove allow shorter two- or three-day hikes.

Orphan Lake with Lake Superior in the distance. You'll find this tiny, gem of a lake for which the trail is named, about 30 m along the trail from the entrance. The lake was named by a family from nearby Agawa Bay who were trappers in the area between the 1930s and 1970s. One winter night, after snowshoeing into the lake two family members were unable to make it back to camp and they stayed at the lake. One of the family remarked that they looked like two lonely orphans, and the name stuck.

This stupendous view of the Lake Superior shore-line is the reward for a short, steep climb to a lookout on the Orphan Lake Trail. In the centre of the photo is Baldhead Beach, the small curved bay that marks the halfway point of the trail. The views are breathtaking, especially on a sunny day when the lake reflects the stunning blue of radiant skies.

Baldhead Beach, the halfway point of Orphan Lake Trail, where it joins up with the Coastal Trail. Unless you hike in, you'll never be able to walk on this beach of multi-coloured pebbles that have been washed smooth by eons of Lake Superior wave action and ice friction. The beach offers an ideal spot for lunch, and an excuse to spend a little time in this special place. An especially good site is at the northerly end, where the Baldhead River enters the lake and the return leg of the trail starts. Some large driftwood provide good seating.

Waterfalls on the Baldhead River are one of the many delights of the Orphan Lake Trail. The path winds its way from the bottom of the falls to the top, and several short side trails enable the hiker to view the falls at various levels. This view shows the top of the falls as the river starts to spill over the rocky ridge.

A hiker pauses to contemplate one of the more challenging sections of the Casque Isles Trail. After leaving remote Lyda Bay, with its lovely sandy beach, the trail re-enters the forest and starts to meander uphill until it reaches this high rocky ridge. From the top of the ridge are fabulous views of Lake Superior and some of the beaches in this area. The trail winds around the cliff edge and then you must descend by way of a wooden ladder.

This view looking north from Eagle Ridge is seldom seen by the casual visitor. Quite unexpectedly the trail emerges onto Eagle Ridge and all the rigors of the trail are forgotten as you savour the breathtaking views from this 300 m high cliff top. You can see the mouth of the famous Nipigon River where it enters Lake Superior. To the north, forested hills roll to infinity. The distant hills at the top of the picture are known as The Palisades, sheer cliffs that draw ice climbers from far and wide in winter.

Sturdy ropes, donated by the local lumber mill and installed by hiking club volunteers, help to make the descent from Eagle Ridge less hazardous, especially when rocks are slippery. After a bit more rock scrambling here and there, the trail continues through swampy ground, passes through some woods and crosses the Stillwater Creek.

Graphite to Hybla

Abandoned Rail Line

- **LENGTH:** 6 km (2 hours) • **DEGREE OF DIFFICULTY:** Easy
- **TYPE OF TRAIL:** Linear • **LOCATION:** Maynooth

HOW TO GET THERE:

Drive Highway 62 to Graphite Road and turn east about 4 km to the old village of Graphite. There is parking by the lake on the south side of Graphite Road. There are two lanes leading off to the south, just west of the lakefront. One is Graphite Lane, the other is a few steps west and is unnamed. This is the one you should take. If car jockeying, park a second car on the Hybla Road, reached from Highway 62 south of the Graphite Road.

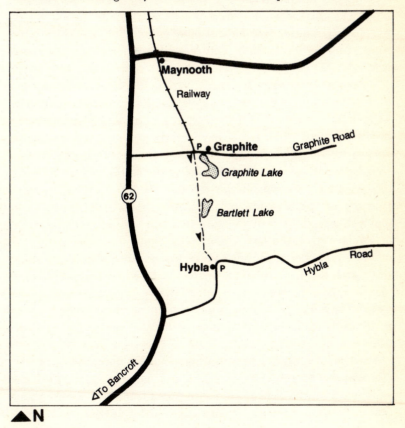

Eastern Ontario

When you walk this trail you are walking a little bit of Ontario's history. This stretch of abandoned rail line is fairly typical of hundreds of similar abandoned rail lines throughout the province. Built to assist in the commerce of the area, they moved lumber, mining materials, people, and goods into areas where few, if any, roads existed. Today they are no longer economical. While that may be bad news for some, for recreationists it represents opportunity. When the tracks have been removed, these wide paths that cut across country can provide access trails for hikers and equestrians. In winter, a number of these old lines become snowmobile and cross-country ski trails.

This particular stretch of line on the edge of the lovely Madawaska Valley was part of the Central Ontario Railway (later Canadian National Railway). It ran from Belleville to Wallace, about 20 km south of Whitney, and was an important transportation route for freight and passengers. The line was a vital support service for the 19th-century lumber industry that flourished around Lake St. Peter.

The lumber industry is considered to be the catalyst that opened up this part of the Madawaska Valley, beginning about 1860. The building of the Central Ontario Railway was largely spearheaded by the discovery of minerals, particularly iron ore, in the Bancroft area to the south. Having gone that far, the lumber industry pushed it as far north as Lake St. Peter. With the coming of the railroad to the Maynooth area, it was possible to ship out logs, lumber, iron ore, graphite, mica, and marble as well as farm products. Canadian National ran a weekly train up the line to its terminal at Wallace until the late 1950s.

You could choose to walk one of any number of sections along this route, but the stretch between Graphite and Hybla is a good one because it runs past a couple of pretty lakes and into a ghost town. There is one stretch, about 500 m north of Hybla, where a stream becomes a swamp after periods of heavy rain and can overflow the trail.

Starting at Graphite, a community named for a mill owned by the National Graphite Company, which closed down in 1919, the trail heads southward running alongside Graphite Lake for about 500 m. This section sees occasional vehicles as there are one or two cottages on this part of the lake. At the southern end of the lake there are wetlands, while woods rise steeply from the west bank. In the soft dirt of the trail, moose tracks are easily visible. There is a feeling of being deep in the wilderness, although the highway is just a few kilometres away.

The wetland drains into a little stream, bordered by wildflowers that flourish in open areas around the track. A forest of black spruce provides a backdrop. The stream disappears and the trail runs through forest once again until it emerges alongside a bay of Graphite Lake. You have now walked about 2 km.

The Graphite Lake shoreline bordering the track is rocky but there are a couple of places where someone wanting to fish could clamber down quite easily.

The trail travels alongside the lake for about 1 km, then follows an embankment that cuts through the edge of the bay. A little farther along where the track leaves the lake there is evidence of fairly recent small-scale logging activity.

Continuing through rockcuts, woods and beside wetlands, the trail crosses over the odd, forgotten railroad tie, until it reaches tiny Bartlett Lake, which it skirts on the west side. It continues on past this into an area blossoming with black-eyed Susans, meadowsweet and fireweed. You can almost imagine being a passenger on the old train and looking out over this little stretch of wilderness.

Shortly before reaching Hybla the trail runs through another swamp. This is where the track can be washed out after heavy rain. At its worst it can be 9 to 10 cm deep and about 40 m wide. Most of this is easily negotiable because you can walk along a small bank at the side of the track, except for about 2 m where the flow sometimes washes out the bank.

Eastern Ontario

None of this concerns a great blue heron, which nonchalantly goes about its business in a corner of the swamp, among the wild irises.

The path continues southward through low banks bordered by sweet-smelling milkweed and white clover, until the landscape flattens out and a building comes into view.

You have now reached the tiny village of Hybla, a community of two churches and a handful of farms. At the turn of the century, Hybla was a flourishing community with a train station, blacksmith's shop and stables, store, ice house, and boarding house. This was an important stop on the long-gone Central Ontario Railway. In the 1920s, the area was the centre of an important feldspar mining industry, with one large mine and 14 small mines operating within a 3-km radius. The feldspar was shipped to the U.S., where it was eagerly snapped up by the glass and ceramic industry. The mines closed in 1935, however the large MacDonald Mine was re-opened briefly in 1955 when it was considered as a possible source of uranium.

Today, the mines, the workers, and the railroad have gone and Hybla is merely a name on the route to a cottage community.

K & P Trail

Lavant Station to Flower Station
Abandoned Rail Line

- **LENGTH:** 14 km (4 to 5 hours) • **DEGREE OF DIFFICULTY:** Easy
- **TYPE OF TRAIL:** Linear • **LOCATION:** Lanark

HOW TO GET THERE:

Take Highway 511 north from Lanark and turn west onto County Road 16. Follow County Road 16 through Poland and Lavant to Lavant Station. The trail goes north from Lavant Station. It is easily identified by the large Conservation Area sign. Parking is available at each end of the trail.

• • •

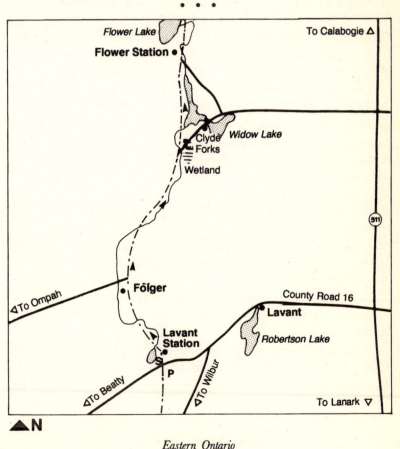

The K & P trail is a 40-km recreational trail operated by the Mississippi Valley Conservation Authority on a portion of an abandoned railway. It takes its name from the old Kingston and Pembroke Railway and is one of a number of abandoned rail lines scattered throughout Ontario that have been turned into recreational trails.

The Kingston and Pembroke Railway was built in the 1870s, operating between the two communities until 1959. Somewhere in its history it was taken over by Canadian Pacific Railway. It was built to transport lumber and other natural resources from the wilderness forests to Kingston on Lake Ontario. It also carried settlers and their supplies north to the wilderness.

A pioneer settlement area that takes pride in a Scottish ancestry, the Lanark area seems little changed today. Farmers still use square-timbered barns that were built to last more than one hundred years ago. There are still residents who remember the days in the 1930s and '40s when the K & P Railway regularly brought in the excise men to locate and dismantle illegal stills operating in the hills.

The last train ran in 1957 and the tracks were removed in 1966. In 1972, the Mississippi Valley Conservation Authority adopted 40 km of it for a recreational trail. The Authority opened it to hikers, mountain bike enthusiasts, off-road vehicles and, in the winter, snowmobilers and skiers. It is even open to automobiles, although the speed limit is 25 kph, so it is not used as a regular thoroughfare.

You can hike the entire 40 km between Snow Road Station in the south and Barryvale in the north if you are so inclined, but if you want to limit your walk to the most pleasant section, this stretch between Lavant Station and Flower Station qualifies. It travels between large, deep rockcuts, past swamps, over a pretty river that runs through a small canyon, and through a particularly beautiful stretch of wetlands. There are lots of opportunities for wildlife viewing.

Starting from Lavant Station, about 10 km north of where the trail starts at Snow Road Station, the trail is easily identified in the village by a large sign. There are one or two houses near the tracks in the village and these give way to paths leading to recreational homes as the trail leaves the village behind. It is very easy to imagine the train rolling out of Lavant Station, picking up speed as the engineer shovelled in the coal. About 500 m along, the trail goes through a large swamp that is part of Graham Lake. There is a backdrop of tall black spruce spearing into the sky, giving the impression of a northern wilderness. Water-lilies add an exotic look to the swamp. Here, too, as in many places in eastern Ontario, the beautiful but destructive purple loosestrife is gaining a firm foothold. A little farther along, some gnawed poplar boughs indicate that a beaver is active in the area.

In another 500 m or so, on higher ground, there is a wooden shelter and privy. Just past this there is a small lake on the left, where, if you are an angler, it may be worth tossing in a line just to test the waters.

After leaving the lake, the trail goes through a high rock cut for about 100 m and the lonely track stretches ahead into tall pines, emerging once again into a swamp area. A goldfinch flits across the path, its colour matched by the gold of the water-lilies flanked by huge lily pads in the swamp.

Every now and again, the gravel on the path parts to reveal old railway ties. The trail cuts directly through the swamp for about 500 m, goes through an area of pines that smell wonderful, then into more swamp. There is a lovely stretch of pines outlined against the horizon on the right at the far side of the swamp.

Passing the swamp, the trail enters a mixed bush and is flanked by the high banks common to railroads. The area here is Crown land and is open to exploration on the numerous trails that lead off the main trail. The trail passes an abandoned homestead with its log barn still pretty much intact.

A stream appears to the right, below the trail, its banks festooned with bright scarlet cardinal flowers. A snake slithers quickly down the path chasing dinner in the form of a frog. The trail runs through an open area where there are hydro pylons, goes back into the bush and then comes to a junction, where there is a Stop sign.

For the next couple of kilometres the trail runs through typical Canadian Shield country—lots of granite rock cuts and mixed forest. There are places here where you can leave the trail and find a rest stop.

About 7 km from the start of the trail you will come to a stone bridge that spans a small, pretty creek some 10 m below the level of the track. Beneath the bridge, the stream churns over a set of rapids between steep rocky banks shaded by hardwoods. The bridge is located in a Crown land access area that is open to exploration, however the steep banks of the river are not easily accessible. Still, it's a very pretty view.

Leaving the small canyon, the trail continues through rockcuts that glisten with mica, and through areas where thick forests line both sides. There is some evidence of ongoing logging operations but nothing that appears extensive. In places the forest opens up and in these areas you can leave the trail if you wish. In these open areas, where the sun can filter through the tree canopy, there are raspberry bushes and patches of blackeyed Susan.

Three km farther on you will come to a lovely wetland, thick with cattails. A couple of mallards rise in quick, graceful flight from lush aquatic grasses. Behind the swamp, willows give way to pines and low-rising hills. Ahead, through the gap in the trees, there is a view of the forested Calabogie mountains. The path cuts through the wetland for about 1 km and re-enters the forest. In another few metres you will glimpse Widow Lake to your right in the distance and finally walk alongside it. There are cottages on the lake, which lend an air of civilization after the wildness of the trail since leaving Lavant Station.

The trail passes the end of the lake and enters the forest again, travelling for about 1 km to reach the end of the trail at Flower Station.

There is a little old-fashioned general store about 50 m to the right on the county road, where you can buy cold drinks and snacks.

Lake St. Peter and Joe's Cabin Trail

Lake St. Peter Provincial Park

- **LENGTH:** 6 to 7 km (2 hours) • **DEGREE OF DIFFICULTY:** Easy
- **TYPE OF TRAIL:** Loop • **LOCATION:** Maynooth

HOW TO GET THERE:

Lake St. Peter Provincial Park is on the east side of Algonquin Park, 45 km north of Bancroft off Highway 127. A short cottage road leads from the highway to the park. Parking is available near the park office. There is a charge for day-use in the provincial park during the operating season, May to September.

• • •

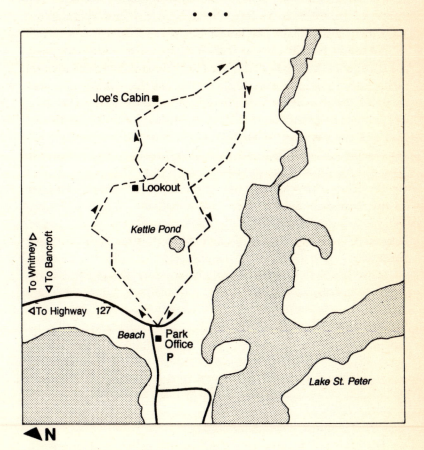

This is a relaxing trail for visitors to cottage country. It leads to a scenic lookout over Lake St. Peter and exposes the hiker to a touch of the history of this part of Ontario by a visit to an old trapper's cabin high in the woods. Although the area was opened up by the lumber industry, Lake St. Peter was a favourite haunt of Group of Seven painters. Both A.Y. Jackson and A.J. Casson made field trips to the area, producing some significant works. The artistic tradition is carried on by several summer art schools that operate in the area.

It is not hard to see why the area attracts landscape artists. The lake is ringed by rugged hills dominated by the mixed forest of the Great Lakes–St. Lawrence forest region, luxuriant with evergreens, maples, white pine and birch. Most of the trail is through a hardwood bush in which maple is the dominant species.

The trail starts directly behind the park office. It starts to climb almost immediately and follows a bit of a switchback for the first 500 m. Near one of the first turns in the trail look for an enormous old tree stump on your left. The stump has a diameter of probably 3 m, providing some idea of the size of the giant white pines that attracted lumber barons to this part of Ontario. The virgin white pine is gone now and many of the early settlements that sprang up around lumber operations are ghost towns.

The trail, flanked by blueberry bushes, continues climbing, gently at first, becoming steeper as it nears the lookout. The forest at this point is a young pine plantation. A chestnut-sided warbler is a welcome sight hopping from branch to branch. As the climb becomes steeper the forest changes to a young hardwood bush and the canopy closes in, providing a shady cover but little in the way of wildflowers. At the point where a blue arrow shows a swing to the left, look straight ahead for an interesting rock formation where there is a small cave. You will swing around the base of this and then start into a very steep climb up a long hill.

At the top of the hill the trail descends slightly and emerges out of the forest onto a flat, rocky plateau. From here there is a viewpoint overlooking two reaches of Lake St. Peter and the hills beyond it. This is the end of the Lookout Trail. The trail to Joe's Cabin starts just beyond the lookout.

The trail to the cabin continues with another steep climb and the hardwood bush closes in. The forest floor is thick with maple seedlings but little else. Here and there signs denote species other than maple, such as black cherry, balsam and yellow birch.

After a final steep climb the path levels out and starts to descend somewhat before crossing a wet spot, which is negotiated by stepping stones. The bush changes here and includes some evergreens and ferns. After climbing a short slope you will emerge into a clearing, which is dominated by the lonely ruins of the deserted cabin. It is roofless now, but it is easy to see that it once was a work of love. The cabin was a large log structure built of hand-hewn logs, dowelled to fit one another. It was built by Joe Goulah, a recluse who depended on his own resources, such as trapping, hunting, and fishing, to keep himself alive. Known locally as "Ole Joe," the recluse reputedly moved here from nearby Mink Lake during the early 1950s where he apparently lived with some 14 dogs, a raccoon, chickens and ducks.

Joe was well known in the area for his handmade lutes and violins, which he crafted from maple and birch grown locally.

It seems that Joe was an independent character. After he became too old to earn his living from trapping, he carved axehandles, which he sold to local lumber companies. He also made miniature canoes and jewellery, but he gave most of these products away.

In the clearing around the cabin are old apple and cherry trees, and also some pillars of stone that Joe Goulah constructed. While they may look like ordinary piles of stone, to Joe these were the Pearly Gates to Heaven, which led from the forest to the clearing around his cabin. This was his Garden of Eden.

The trail crosses the clearing to reach the return path and re-enters the forest. It is eerily quiet. Is that the wind sighing in the tree-tops, or is it Ole Joe's ghost hovering around the spot he loved so much?

The trail descends quite steeply and then enters a pine plantation. There are two or three wet spots to negotiate before you reach a small, deep, kettle lake ringed by pines, with maple woods rising steeply behind. A number of fairly large trees that have been dropped by beavers indicate there is an active colony around here. From the kettle lake there is a short steep climb out of the depression, followed by a brief walk through a young forest to return to the park office.

Eastern Ontario

Petroglyphs and High Falls

- **LENGTH:** 13 km (4+ hours) • **DEGREE OF DIFFICULTY:** Moderate
- **TYPE OF TRAIL:** Linear • **LOCATION:** Peterborough

HOW TO GET THERE:

This trail starts in Petroglyphs Provincial Park and travels into the Peterborough Crown Game Preserve. The park entrance is located 55 km northeast of Peterborough, 11 km east of Highway 28 on Northey's Bay Road. Enter the park gates and drive to the parking lot closest to the Petroglyphs site. A park brochure outlines the trails but is not particularly helpful. Follow the High Falls trail signs.

• • •

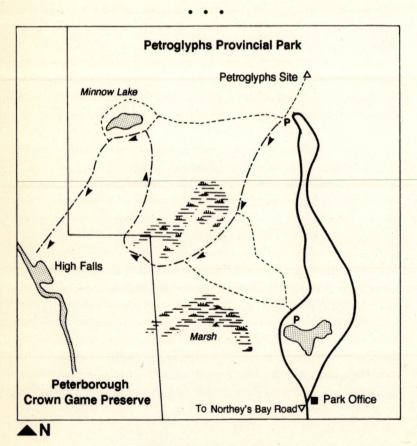

Petroglyphs Provincial Park houses one of the most important archaeological sites in Canada and is a sacred place to members of the Ojibwa Anishnabe Nation. The several hundred carvings that cover the face of some large smooth rocks here are believed to have been carved between 500 and 1,000 years ago by the Algonkians. The peoples of the First Nations call them "the rocks that teach" because it is believed they carry lessons for all peoples.

This mysticism carries over into the trails that run through the woods close to where the symbols were carved. Walking through the forest it is not hard to envision why the Algonkians chose this place as a sacred site. It is a place of sheer beauty with its pine forests, tiny perfect lakes, and wetlands.

The Peterborough Crown Game Preserve is also a place of some note. A magnificent wilderness of more than 15,000 ha, it is home to hundreds of white-tailed deer.

Before starting the trail you may wish to visit the interpretive centre to view the petroglyphs. The centre is located close to the parking lot, near the start of the trail. A huge rock that bears the most significant figures and symbols is now protected from the elements by a large glass building. Knowledgeable interpreters stand by ready to answer questions. Ojibwa elders occasionally visit the site to perform sacred ceremonies, leaving gifts of tobacco here and there among the carvings.

Start the trail from the parking lot and follow the path to a large map which details various trails. Walk down the hill and go in the direction signified by orange and yellow disks. The path will be marked "High Falls" and it leads into a forest of white pines, spaced to allow lots of sunlight, which dapples the forest floor, highlighting the ferns and scarlet fruit of the bunchberry. It also encourages such wildflowers as the pretty blue knapweed, coreopsis and the orchid helleborine. The path travels up and down over numerous small ridges until it reaches a boardwalk over a marsh. Patches of jewelweed brush their orange heads against you as you cross. Some small turtles sun themselves on logs, which seems right, somehow, since the turtle is the park's symbol, and a major feature of the ancient carvings. The carvers believed the turtle carried the weight of the earth on its back.

The path continues on through grassy areas and back into the gentle beauty of a mixed forest. Scattered here and there along the trail are cairn-like structures. These bear reproductions of the mystical carvings—turtles, canoes, and the teacher Nanabush. The originals are housed under the glass roof of the park's interpretive centre.

Still following orange and yellow signs, the path comes to a wetland, sparkling with white water-lilies and spanned by another wooden boardwalk. At this point, the orange trail splits to go to the West Day Use picnic area. The yellow trail to High Falls goes off to the right and into a pine forest where Minnow Lake can be glimpsed through the trees to your right. The lake, ringed by tall white pines, is almost too perfect. On a high point overlooking it are the ruins of an old log cabin. Some large rock outcroppings offer good rest spots and it is tempting to examine them to see if there are carvings that might have missed discovery.

A path called the Trail of Nanabush circles the lake. This is a self-interpretive trail that reveals how the porcupine got its quills and where white water-lilies came from. You can include this as part of your hike, or you can bypass it.

After passing the swamp at the west end of Minnow Lake the trail markers change to blue and the trail dips slightly south on its way to High Falls. After clambering down a ledge and then up a hill you will leave the provincial park and enter the Peterborough Crown Game Preserve.

The trail through the preserve becomes more rugged, moving from forests of white pine and onto high rocky plateaus where a lizard may skitter across your path.

The path is easy to follow as it is well worn and blue disk trail markers are nailed to trees here and there. Parts of the trail wind through pine forests that smell wonderfully pungent, something like a wild blueberry pie baking in the oven. There are several challenges in the form of wetlands that must be crossed. No boardwalks here—just some old tree trunks placed side by side across the wet spots. One, in particular, crosses a wide swamp, another quite memorable crossing is over what appears to be a log jam over a small canyon.

After crossing the latter, keep a lookout for poison ivy that is growing on some of the rocks. You may inadvertently place a hand on some as you lever yourself over. About 500 m from here you will enter a hardwood forest and soon a small lake will appear on your left. On your right is a moss-covered cliff. The path travels between the cliff and the lake until it turns for an easy climb up the cliff. You will emerge onto a rocky plateau and soon will hear the sound of the falls.

Walk across the plateau to reach the head of the falls. It is a pretty spot. The waters of Eel's Creek tumble several metres over the rocks in a series of falls and rapids. You can sit in the shade of the cedars on huge rocks overlooking the falls to eat lunch. Again, watch out for poison ivy.

You must return to Petroglyphs Provincial Park taking the same paths through the Peterborough Crown Game Preserve that you took on the way in. Once you reach provincial park property some small diversions may be taken to vary the route back to the parking lot.

Bruce-Georgian Bay

REGIONAL OVERVIEW

THIS LOVELY region is dominated by Lake Huron and Georgian Bay, as well as by the Niagara Escarpment. It includes the Bruce Peninsula with its more than 800 km of shoreline and some of the best stretches of the Bruce Trail. It also encompasses the great sweep of Nottawasaga Bay, the fabulous Beaver Valley and Collingwood's Blue Mountains.

The major hiking opportunities are on the Bruce Trail and in some of the many Niagara Escarpment parks and conservation areas it passes through. Other excellent hiking is on the Midland section of the Ganaraska Trail. One section leads into the **Wye Marsh** near Midland and there are also lovely trails in the Wye Marsh facility itself.

A number of conservation areas offer hiking opportunities, many associated or looped with the Bruce Trail. These include **Old Baldy**, **Rocklyn Creek** and **Walters Falls**, all not far from Kimberley. **Inglis Falls** and **West Rocks** are in the Owen Sound area. Information on all of these properties is available from the Grey–Sauble Conservation Authority at (519) 376-3076.

There is also hiking at **Spirit Rock Conservation Area** north of Wiarton on the east side of Highway 6 and this, too, is managed by the Grey–Sauble Conservation Authority.

Farther north on the highway, at Dorcas Bay, the Federation of Ontario Naturalists owns the **Dorcas Bay Reserve** where hikers can walk through coniferous forests and along the Lake Huron shoreline. More than 15 orchid species grow in the reserve. It is located on the west side of Highway 6, adjacent to the Bruce National Park's **Singing Sands Beach**. Another Federation property is at **Petrel Point** where unusual wildflowers grow in a shoreline fen next to Lake Huron. To reach it, follow Highway 6 to Mar where you will turn west. Continue to a T-junction, then drive north about 3 km until you come to a small road running west. The road divides the northern and southern halves of the reserve. Other nearby interesting spots include the **Oliphant Fen**, about 15 km south on the beach road. Obtain more information from the Federation of Ontario Naturalists at (416) 444-9866.

There are some abandoned railroad opportunities in the Bruce Peninsula area, but trails have not been developed so far. If you don't mind walking on the tracks, there is a pretty stretch from **Allenford to Hepworth**, which travels through the scenic hills around Park Head. Access this from County Road 21, just west of Highway 6 at Allenford, then head north on the tracks.

From Tobermory, at the top of the Bruce Peninsula you can take a boat ride to **Flowerpot Island**, part of Parks Canada's National Marine Park, where there are hiking opportunities.

Parks Canada also offers wonderful hiking opportunities on **Beausoleil Island** off Honey Harbour on the east side of Georgian Bay. The park offers some 30 km of trails on the island, 2 km from the mainland, which is reached by water taxi. More information on Beausoleil Island trails is available by calling Parks Canada in Honey Harbour at (705) 756-2415.

In the Collingwood–Meaford area there are 49 km of trails in the 1,825-ha **Kolapore Uplands Resource Management Area**. The trails were developed for use by cross-country skiers, but are available to hikers when there is no snow. To reach the area go north on Highway 24 from Highway 89. Just before you reach Singhampton, turn west onto Highway 4, and then north on County Road 2. Where County Road 2 takes a big swing to the west and then starts going north again, park and look for an orange blaze on the west side of the road. There is another access point just north of the village of Kolapore farther north on Highway 2. Obtain more information from the Grey–Sauble Conservation Authority.

An abandoned rail line has been put to excellent use in the

Collingwood area. The **Georgian Trail** is a 32-km path between the towns of Meaford and Collingwood that has been developed by the municipality for use by hikers and cyclists. For more information call the Collingwood Parks & Recreation Department at (705) 445-1030.

Trails of Awenda Provincial Park

- **LENGTH**: 13 km (4+ hours) • **DEGREE OF DIFFICULTY**: Easy
- **TYPE OF TRAIL**: Loop • **LOCATION**: Penetanguishene

HOW TO GET THERE:

Follow Highway 93 to Penetanguishene on Georgian Bay. Turn left (west) on Robert Street and follow it to Highway 26. Drive north on Highway 26 and follow provincial park signs to a cottage road leading east. Still following the signs, turn left (north) from the cottage road and into the park entrance. The park charges a day-use fee during the operating season, which is early May to

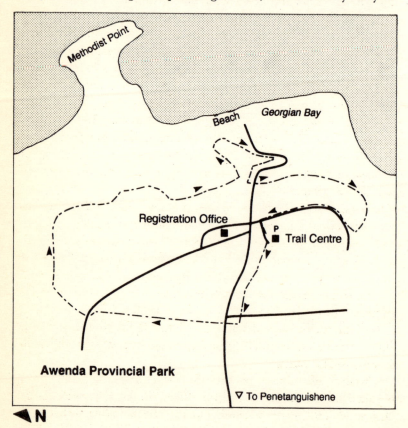

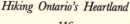

late September; and December to March for cross-country skiing. The trails can be accessed when the park is not in operation.

. . .

The beauty of Awenda trails—and Awenda really is beautiful—is that you can tailor your hike to either long or short, or to include one area rather than another. It's a wonderful place for a walk in the forest to savour the sights, sounds, and smells of the various seasons. It is hard to say when it is most attractive. In summer you can break your hike with a swim from a lovely beach. In spring, the just-born green of mixed hardwoods is alive with songbirds. Trilliums, showy lady's slipper, false Solomon's seal, wild ginger and violets warm the heart with their promise.

The fall, in this 1,935-ha forest, is just the place for a brisk ramble among the glorious reds, golds and russets of the hardwoods.

If this weren't enough, there are great views overlooking Georgian Bay, and lots of opportunities for wildlife viewing. Creatures such as the great blue heron, deer, and smaller mammals are frequently seen. As for historic attractions, the 13-km Bluff Trail partially follows the upper edge of the Nipissing Bluff, a raised beach created 5500 years ago by glacial Lake Nipissing. There are believed to be at least 17 archaeological sites left behind by the four different cultures that have inhabited the area over the past 11,000 years.

It is somewhat of a shock, however, to eat lunch and survey the summer activity on a lovely beach and realize that in 1632, Etienne Brûlé, explorer and mapper of the Great Lakes, was executed here by the Wendat peoples of the Huron Nation for what they believed was treachery in trading activities. Perhaps ironically, or maybe not, the name Awenda is a loosely translated Wendat word meaning roughly "you can trust me, I am your friend."

Awenda invites exploration today. The only fly in the ointment appears to be an abundant crop of poison ivy, so it is advisable to stay on the paths.

A total of five interconnecting trails start from the trail centre, not far from the park registration office. Some trails, such as the Dunes, which leads to a scenic lookout, the Wendat, a historical trail around Second Lake, and the Beach, a linear trail leading to four beaches, are served by parking areas close to the trail access points. Bear in mind that you may not be able to access these trails without a long walk from the park entrance when the park is not in operation.

The trail covered here is an approximate 9-km loop heading southwest from the trail centre using the Bluff Trail (blue markers), turning westwards onto the Brûlé Trail (green markers), turning north by picking up the Bluff Trail again, and traversing the Bluff edge until it intersects with the Beach Trail. It then takes the Beach Trail down the bluff, returning via the park road, then picking up the Bluff Trail again to go back to the trail centre.

From the trail centre, where there are privies, the Bluff Trail enters a pleasant, leafy, hardwood forest using a wide, well-packed sandy trail. Many of the trails follow old logging roads established in the late 1800s when logs were taken to the shore and rafted to mills in Penetanguishene and Midland.

Follow this south for some 600 m crossing a park road. A few metres south of here the trail turns west onto the Brûlé Trail, following green markers. Turn right onto this trail, cross the main north-south road through the park, and enter the forest again. Growing in clusters close to the path is squawroot, an interesting plant that is parasitic to the roots of the oak tree. The plants flower in spring but in summer the plants are reminiscent of corn cobs, or pine cones.

Masses of pink-mauve knapweed, Queen Anne's lace, yellow mullein and evening primrose are a colourful border to the park roads. Underneath the trees are purple bergamot, pink tick trefoil and helleborine orchid. Mushrooms are numerous and colourful.

The trail passes the northern edge of the Bear campground area and comes to another park road. Here, the Brûlé Trail connects with the Dunes Trail and once again with the Bluff Trail. Leaving the Brûlé Trail, follow the blue markers of the Bluff Trail and bear left for about 50 m, then turn right and cross the road to where there is a map. Follow the blue signs into the woods.

This path skirts the edge of Deer campground as it travels northwards. A huge bluff is to your left. Past the campgrounds the trail continues for almost 2 km, eventually coming within sight of the lake, although not much can be seen in leaf season. When the path intersects with the Beach Trail it heads some 32 m down the face of the bluff using a series of 155 steps. When you reach the lower level the change in the ecosystem is immediately apparent. From gentle hardwoods, the trail now runs for a short way through a swampy area of cedars and hemlock. Enormous boulders lie around the path.

The trail crosses the road and soon opens onto a small sandy beach. A good stop for lunch and a summer swim.

From the beach you can see Methodist Point, which is the point of land curving to the west, and beyond it are Christian, Beckwith and Hope islands. To your immediate right is Giant's Tomb Island and on the far right are the beach areas around Honey Harbour.

Retrace your steps from the beach and turn left onto the park road, passing a small pond where there are great blue herons. The road ascends the bluff and walks roughly south for some 700 m before intersecting with the Bluff Trail. Turn left into the woods and follow the blue markers.

After walking about 1 km through the forest, the lake may be glimpsed through the trees lining the edge of the bluff to your left. When you reach the park road again, turn right and follow the road past the turn-off to the park administration office, and on back to the trail centre parking lot.

Cape Croker Loop

Cape Croker Reserve

- **LENGTH:** 8 km (3 hours) • **DEGREE OF DIFFICULTY:** Moderate
- **TYPE OF TRAIL:** Loop • **LOCATION:** Wiarton

HOW TO GET THERE:

Take Highway 6 north of Wiarton. Turn right onto Bruce County Road 9 past the village of Colpoys. Turn right onto Township Road 18 (Purple Valley Road) and follow it as it turns north. Take the second entrance east into the Cape Croker Reserve and follow the signs to Cape Croker Park. Drive towards the escarpment and before you reach the campground you will crest a hill overlooking

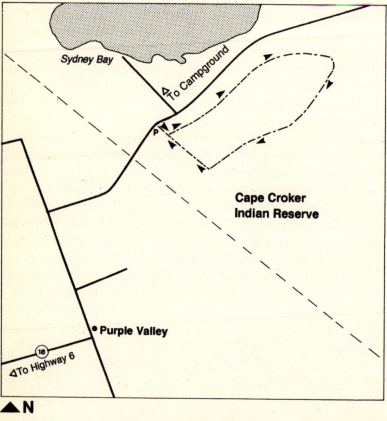

Sydney Bay. Park on the shoulder of the road just over the crest of the hill and past a road sign signalling a steep hill. Walk about 500 m from your vehicle towards the bay and look for the trail entrance on your right (south side). Since you are on the Cape Croker Reserve, which is private land, it would be gracious to leave a note on your windshield indicating your name, address and phone number, that you are hiking, and when you expect to return. The trail is actually part of the Bruce Trail (known as the Jones Bluff Side Trail) and permission has been granted for hiking across it.

• • •

The trail you are about to follow was made not by the thick soles of hiking boots, but by centuries of footsteps made by the soft moccasins of Canada's First Nations people. This hike around Jones Bluff on the Niagara Escarpment is one of the few historic First Nations walking trails in Ontario. It follows a route that Ojibwa families walked on summer afternoons. This is a place for lovers and a setting for family picnics. With its long, sweeping vistas of water, land and sky, it has also doubtlessly been a place for communing with the natural forces and spirits that control these elements of the earth.

This is a trail that goes high in the sky, its heights resembling the mesas of the American southwest. It is a safe bet that at one time these heights were used as vantage points by the lookouts responsible for the safety of the village. Think, then, of the respect that Ontario's native peoples held for this land as you walk the trail. This is not a walk to be hurried. It is a place to stop and smell the wildflowers, savour the views, and marvel at the beauty of this special part of the Bruce Peninsula. For an experience that is close to mystical, enjoy it on a Thanksgiving weekend, when the air is cool and crisp, and a brilliant fall sun turns the waters of Georgian Bay to cobalt blue and the forested hills to a palette of russet, bronze, yellow and green.

The Bruce Trail now follows the route started by those moccasins. Look for the familiar white blaze on a tree off the highway where the trail starts. From here you follow a well-worn trail lined with old fencing. The trail heads southeast and immediately starts into a gentle climb for about 150 m, passing an open field on the right.

When you come to a fork, take the path to the left that is marked with a white blaze. The path that leads due south, marked by a blue blaze, is where the loop route returns at the end of the walk. The trail is well blazed and well maintained.

Follow the trail to the left as it enters the forest and starts to climb up the escarpment. The forest floor is typically Niagara Escarpment terrain with its rocks and boulders. Limestone terraces are hung with ferns and other greenery. The trail continues to climb, twisting around the rocks, and after about 15 minutes reaches the first lookout. The view is sublime. You can walk right to the edge of the escarpment for a view of Sydney Bay, and beyond to a great sweep of Georgian Bay and over to Barrier Island. The island is also part of the Cape Croker community and many residents go there to fish. Spread out below you are the scattered houses of the community, while to the north you can see Cape Dundas and Gun Point jutting into the blue waters of Georgian Bay.

Leaving the first lookout, the trail continues close to the edge of the escarpment, crossing a number of deep fissures in the rock. There are frequent lookouts over the water from rocky promontories, and these make excellent lunch stops. It is incredibly beautiful.

This part of the escarpment is a remarkably rich ecosystem. You can spot many birds, such as goldfinches, yellow warblers, cardinals and dozens of that cheeky denizen of the forest—the chickadee. Wildflowers include the gorgeous scarlet-tipped painted cup, known locally as Indian paintbrush. From the top of the escarpment you can look down and watch hawks and turkey vultures riding the thermal air currents up towards you. On some days, if you are patient, one of those thermal riders could be an osprey.

If you do it fast, this walk along the northeast cliff face will take about 45 minutes, but take your time. This is one trail that begs the hiker to slow down, to marvel and enjoy. The trail meanders on, climbing up and down over small ridges and limestone terraces. At times it passes through undulating meadows that look like perfectly planned Japanese gardens with small shrubs, junipers and ferns.

When the trail finally leaves the cliff edge, the terrain flattens out into a steady, easy walk atop the escarpment. Walk along this trail for about 15 minutes until you come to Jones Bluff at the easternmost tip of the trail. It is not known why it is called Jones Bluff, but there are many families of that name living in the Cape Croker community. The view from here is a spectacular vista of both Sydney Bay to the north and the long narrow inlet that is Colpoy's Bay to the south. The islands you can see are Hay, White Cloud and Griffin.

Hay Island was settled in the 1920s by two Hungarian brothers who brought some European wild boar and let them loose on the island. The descendants of those original boar survive on the island today.

On the second leg of the hike, the trail winds through a mature hardwood forest with lots of oak trees. The canopy is so dense that little light reaches the forest floor. The walking is easy, and after about 15 minutes the trail emerges onto a rocky promontory that offers excellent views of Colpoy's Bay. If you haven't had lunch, this is one of the better spots on the trail.

From here the trail winds through large meadows where wild grapes grow, and then it comes back out onto the cliff overlooking Colpoy's Bay and follows the cliff top for a short way. After turning away from the cliff edge for the last time and crossing some meadows, the trail intersects with an old logging road, marked by blue blazes. Turn right and follow the logging road back to the highway.

Little Cove to Cyprus Lake

Bruce Peninsula—Georgian Bay
Bruce Trail

• **LENGTH:** 15 km (6 hours) • **DEGREE OF DIFFICULTY:** Challenging
• **TYPE OF TRAIL:** Linear • **LOCATION:** Tobermory

HOW TO GET THERE:

The recommended approach is to park your car at the Head of Trails in Bruce Peninsula National Park off Highway 6, south of Tobermory and arrange a drop-off at Little Cove, about 12 km north on Highway 6. Turn right onto Little Cove and follow the

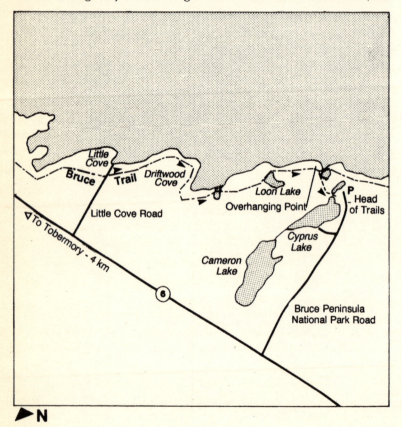

gravel road to the Georgian Bay shoreline. The trail, marked with Bruce Trail white blazes, goes off to the right.

• • •

If you could imagine the perfect trail—challenging, but with delightful rewards of spectacular views, this would probably be it. You will encounter strange and wonderful rock formations, cliffs, mysterious caves, holes in the ground that you can climb down, glimpses of water so clear it takes the breath away and white beaches that dazzle your eyes. What more could a hiker possibly want!

There can be few hikes anywhere that rival the scenery to be found on this remote stretch of the Bruce Peninsula that juts like an upside down leg and foot into the blue waters of Lake Huron and Georgian Bay. The terminus of the famed Bruce Trail that traces the ragged lines of the Niagara Escarpment for more than 700 km is at Tobermory, 5 km west of here. The 30 km of the Bruce Trail that extends east and south from Tobermory is considered to be the most challenging and dangerous of the entire route.

The section described here hugs the stretch of Georgian Bay shoreline at the very top of the Peninsula, running roughly west to east, before it starts its long journey southwards. Georgian Bay is one of Ontario's "great" lakes, and it isn't nicknamed the big "Blue Water" for nothing. Viewed from the trail on a sunny day, its great blue expanse is breathtaking. From the cliff edge you can look down and see huge limestone boulders that have tumbled some 30 metres or more from the cliff face, where they rest just below the surface of the water, like jewels in an azure setting. Everything looks filmed in technicolour. Offshore, dark green-topped islands are ringed with white and washed with cobalt blue. Along the shore, white cliffs are capped with evergreens. And these marvelous views, these glimpses of dramatic, lonely shoreline, are not accessible by road, so hikers are the major beneficiaries as they follow the trail along the cliff edge.

It was this kind of beauty, and its accompanying plantlife, that caused the Niagara Escarpment to be named a World Biosphere Reserve in 1990.

The section of the Bruce Trail outlined here starts at Little Cove, a breathtakingly lovely small inlet with a white pebble beach often frequented by divers. This is one of the best places for beginners to gain experience in this area. The Bruce Peninsula is the home of Canada's only national marine park, known as Fathom Five National Park.

Be sure to stay on the east side of the beach because the other side is private property. There is limited parking.

Easily found from the bush road, the trail starts just short of the beach and is marked with a white blaze. It immediately enters a dense forest of cedar and balsam sprinkled with aspen and birch. The path is wide at this point and extremely well maintained, thanks to faithful Bruce Trail members. The trail climbs steadily upwards and the hiker is soon rewarded with views of the lake out towards Bear's Rump Island and the larger Flowerpot Island.

If you look along the cliff edge of the mainland you can see a small flowerpot, easily spotted by its characteristic shape and topping of greenery. This is a smaller version of the prominent flowerpot shapes found on Flowerpot Island.

The trail climbs steadily and becomes more rugged underfoot, varying from rough, but fairly flat limestone pavement to a series of strange, rocky ridges that stick up like plates standing on edge. Occasionally you will find yourself climbing down into gullies, only to climb back out again in short order. On parts of the trail, huge limestone boulders form walls along the route with cedars and evergreens clinging in crevices. On other parts, narrow, but long caves are topped by enormous overhanging rocks. With this type of terrain hiking boots are a must. Don't try it wearing sneakers.

Boots also offer some protection against the Massassauga rattlesnake, which does live in this area. However, the creature is very shy and will avoid you if it can.

After about 20 minutes on the trail you can stand near the cliff edge and look back along the line of the cliffs towards the village of Tobermory where, if you are there at the right time, you may see the ferry that plies between Tobermory and Manitoulin Island. The lighthouse at Tobermory is quite easy to pick out.

The cliff edge along this stretch is home to some of the oldest trees in Canada. Ancient stunted cedars, possibly 600 to 800 years old, cling precariously to the sides of the cliffs. These, because of the remoteness of the area, were identified only a short time ago.

Some 45 minutes after leaving Little Cove, you will come upon a lookout point that offers a view of a tall, jutting piece of cliff down to your left. Look closely towards the base and you will notice a cave through which a stream appears to be flowing.

The trail continues along the top of the escarpment through thick forests, eventually obscuring your view of the lake. Now the walking becomes easier, with packed earth underfoot. At times the trail passes through great stretches of once-logged areas where thin soils barely cover the limestone pavement. This is the least picturesque part of the trail, but interesting because of the widely differing ecosystems it passes through, from meadows to coarsely-grassed areas liberally sprinkled with low juniper bushes.

This part of the Bruce Peninsula was heavily logged in the late 1800s, when as many as six lumber kings harvested the white pine for ships and hemlock for turpentine.

Although you probably won't notice it as you walk, the trail makes a big sweep around the bay known as Driftwood Cove. The trail comes down to the shoreline at its southernmost point and emerges onto a large pebble beach. Follow the shoreline until you see the white blaze in the trees that marks the continuation of the trail back into the bush.

The trail now picks up an old forestry track for a short way. Look carefully for a trail marker here because it is easy to miss. You will make a turn to the left and soon will be climbing gently once more to the top of the escarpment, heading eastward through a pine forest. For a while, pine needles underfoot make a pleasant change from rocks.

It doesn't last. Soon the trail leads over rocky ridges again as it heads in an easterly direction towards Loon Lake. Here you will probably experience an overpowering urge to cool off your feet, but the shoreline is not easily negotiable. Shortly after passing the lake the trail leads down a rocky miniature canyon to the slab beach of Georgian Bay.

Follow the trail as it winds back to the top of the escarpment and you will shortly arrive at Overhanging Rock. This can be viewed from a promontory slightly to the west and must be seen to be believed. As its name implies, this is an enormous headland with an overhang of something like 12 metres. There is literally nothing but water below it. This is a huge chunk of coral reef left over from the shallow inland sea that once covered this land. Erosion here is ongoing and you can actually see flowerpots in the making. Flowerpots are formed when waves and ice erode the soft limestone cliffs, separating chunks of the cliff into freestanding rock pillars. With a topping of cedar greenery, the rock pillars become "flowerpots."

Some 10 m inland you will find a hole in the ground, marked by two white blazes, where you can descend to explore the base of Overhanging Rock. Some call this "Hillary's Hole" in the mistaken belief that it was used by Everest explorer Sir Edmund Hillary, while practicing for his conquest of the mountain.

The rock you are standing on is dolomite, formed more than 400 million years ago. It contains magnesium from the ancient sea water, which prevents it from eroding away as fast as limestone and allows the slower rate of erosion to fashion it into picturesque shapes.

You are now nearing the last leg of the trail and soon will emerge onto a boulder beach. Here, a trail leads upwards along an old stream bed, passing Marr Lake and leading on to Cyprus Lake. Alternatively, you can continue farther east along the Bruce Trail towards Indian Head Cove and the Grotto. As for us, we'll leave that for another day and head for home, by car.

Devil's Glen and Nottawasaga Bluffs

The Bruce Trail

- **LENGTH:** 12 km (4.5 hours)
- **DEGREE OF DIFFICULTY:** Moderate to challenging
- **TYPE OF TRAIL:** Linear • **LOCATION:** Glen Huron

HOW TO GET THERE:

Take Highway 24 to Devil's Glen Provincial Park and park either in the park or on the road shoulder. Then drive a second car to Simcoe County Road 62. Go through the village of Glen Huron and turn west onto Nottawasaga Sideroad (SR 12-13). Travel 2.6

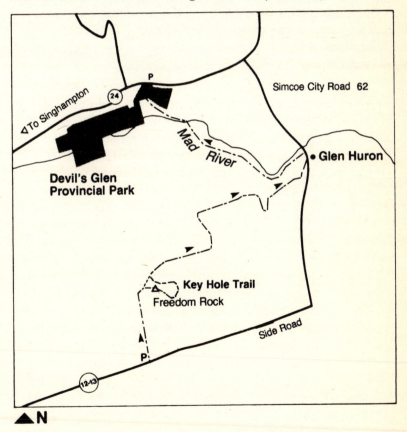

km and park on the grass shoulder opposite a sideroad heading southward.

• • •

If you like to explore unusual places you are in for a treat on this trail. You will squeeze through a small opening in a wall of rock and walk through a deep, cold canyon where snow remains well into summer. You can also visit Freedom Rock, a towering crag that has separated from the main cliff face of the Niagara Escarpment. Freedom Rock bears the scars of now-disappearing political slogans carved at some time in the past.

Other riches on this trail include uncommon plants such as the unusual pink coralroot orchid, the yellow ladyslipper orchid and the rare hart's-tongue fern. There are also a couple of outstanding views and the grand finale is a muscle-straining climb up what seems like a thousand steps from the valley floor of Devil's Glen. In reality there are probably only about 500.

As this is a linear trail you will need to arrange a drop off or shuttle arrangement, parking one car at the end of the trail in Devil's Glen Provincial Park. (If this is not possible, you can follow a short loop trail from Singhampton to Freedom Rock and the Keyhole Trail. Alternatively, you can park in Devil's Glen Provincial Park and hike only the Mad River Loop.)

To follow the linear trail that takes in all of these attractions, start from Nottawasaga Sideroad 12-13 on the north side of the road. This side trail of the Bruce Trail follows a road allowance between farm fields before the trail narrows and heads into a mixed bush. The trail crosses a stream at the bottom of a small valley and comes to a junction. Take the fork to the right. This trail continues through an area of bush and then becomes quite rocky underfoot. In the woods at the edge of the trail are yellow lady slipper orchids and columbines. Before long you will see a prominent sign for the Keyhole Trail. This was erected by the Nottawasaga Valley Conservation Authority, which owns this part of the land.

There's no mistaking the keyhole. A solid wall of rock offers an opening just wide enough for an average person to squeeze through, provided you can contort yourself into a bit of an angle.

The best way seems to be to put your left leg through the crevice and then bend your body, face down and ease yourself through. Don't raise your head while doing this, though, since there is a nasty overhang.

Once through the keyhole the climate change is remarkable. On a sunny 22°C day, we found the temperature inside the small canyon to be just above the freezing mark. The long, narrow L-shaped canyon has moss-covered walls some 30 m high. After exploring, you exit by a steep but easy climb just to the right of the crevice where you entered.

Your next stop will be Freedom Rock and you will need to look carefully for this as the entrance to it is hidden and easily missed. Follow the trail, which continues to climb up through the woods, until it is obvious that you are close to the edge of the escarpment. Then start looking for a double yellow blaze on a tree on the escarpment side. A path goes sharply down the side of the cliff. It is very slippery, even in dry weather, and you will need to choose your footing carefully. It may be unwise to attempt it in wet weather.

You can get right to the base of this towering 60-m-high rock and walk around two sides of it. The slogans are there, as promised, but they are hard to read now. What we didn't expect was a clump of brilliant scarlet peonies that someone had planted at its base, either as some sort of tribute, or as a touch of whimsy.

The climb back up to the trail on top of the escarpment is about as challenging as climbing down. Back on top, the trail continues threading its way along the thickly wooded edge of the escarpment. The next point of interest is a campsite maintained by the Nottawasaga Valley Conservation Authority and there are privies here.

Cross the campsite and take the right fork, which passes through a field and then re-enters the bush. At the next fork, go to the left, following white trail signs. This leads through a young hardwood bush to an old logging road, crosses it at an angle slightly to the right, and heads into the forest again. After crossing the forest, the path runs alongside some incredibly deep gullies for about 200 m or more. Follow the edge of the escarpment, cross a natural bridge to your left, and you will find yourself on the edge of a wide plateau on top of the escarpment. This is an excellent rest stop or lunch break, with a few well-placed rocks for seats, and long, lovely views of the rural landscape to the southwest. Turkey vultures ride the thermal air currents below. You will now have been hiking about 1 hour and 30 minutes.

Leaving the escarpment, take the path that leads from the middle of the plateau and continue straight ahead for about 500 m. Watch for the double blaze on the trees that denotes a left turn, which will return you to the conservation authority campsite.

When you get to the campsite, cross over it and head for the right hand corner of the clearing, following the white markers. This trail leads on through the woods until it intersects with a trail marked by a blue blaze. Do not turn here. The blue-blazed trail leads to a Bruce Trail parking lot in Singhampton, allowing access to the area by a shorter, looped trail.

The white-blazed Bruce Trail weaves on through woods, carpeted by wild lily-of-the-valley and white violets, until it ends at a wooden stile over a fence. There is a rather curiously placed "Bruce Trail Area Parking" sign on the fence. Ignore this as it actually refers to the Singhampton parking area.

Once over the stile, the trail travels through a pretty meadow where turkey vultures circle low overhead. It passes through another meadow, past some old farmhouse ruins and then enters a hardwood bush. Keep your eyes open for enormous old maples alongside the trail.

The trail winds through the woods for about 2 km, climbing ridges and looking down over acres of green carpeted forest. When you come to a gravel road, turn right. The road offers easy walking for about 1 km then, as you crest a hill, a glorious panorama spreads out before you. You can see the great curve of Nottawasaga Bay, with a view of the world's longest freshwater beach— Wasaga—and the lovely neighbouring beaches that sweep the western curve of the bay.

You are now roughly at the half-way point of your hike and there is a good rest stop on the wide grass shoulders. You may even be lucky enough to spot a Baltimore oriole here.

The road continues down the side of the escarpment, approaching a patchwork quilt of farm fields. The main Bruce Trail goes off to the left, heading for Devil's Glen via the steep ski hills of the Devil's Glen Ski Club. Our trail continues down the road, dropping quite steeply now. At the bottom of the hill where there is parking for a couple of cars you can look below and see the Mad River.

Follow the road for about 5 km to where it meets the Glen Huron Road. Turn left and walk downhill and through the tiny village. On your left you will see the Hamilton Brothers sawmill. The trail, marked by blue blazes, cuts along the side of the sawmill, past an old dam and mill pond, until it threads alongside the chattering Mad River.

Approaching Devil's Glen Ski Club, go past the snow-making ponds, alongside the power house and cross the main yard, turning right between the lodge and the ski shop. Cross the bridge over the river, go through the parking lot and turn back into the bush on your left. Watch your footing along the path because there are exposed tree roots. It is marshy and very muddy after rain, however there are numerous boardwalks. Keep your eyes open for the rare hart's-tongue fern.

When you get to a fork which points to the Mad River Loop, keep to your right and take a deep breath. This is the start of the long climb up the escarpment to the top of the valley. The wooden steps hinder, rather than help in the ascent, but they do save the trail from erosion. About half-way up, a stunning little waterfall threads its way down the escarpment. It could not look more perfect if it had been landscaped for a garden.

More steps, more climbing, and just when you think you can't cope with one more, voila, the top of the Niagara Escarpment and you are at trail's end in Devil's Glen Provincial Park.

Bruce Peninsula National Park

Georgian Bay–Marr Lake Trail

- **LENGTH:** 3 km (2 hours)
- **DEGREE OF DIFFICULTY:** Easy to moderate
- **TYPE OF TRAIL:** Loop • **LOCATION:** Tobermory

HOW TO GET THERE:

This trail is located in the Cyprus Lake area of Bruce Peninsula National Park, off Highway 6, 18 km south of Tobermory.

• • •

This trail is strictly for sightseeing. The Georgian Bay coastline here is a perfect example of the dramatic scenery that results from

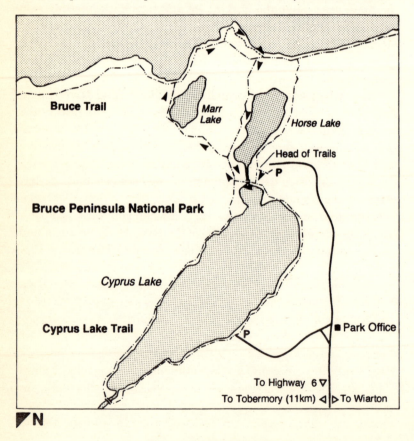

erosion of dolomitic limestone by centuries of pounding waves and scouring ice. This short section of coastline is riddled with caves and natural bridges. Thousand-year-old cedars cling tenaciously to tortured cliffs, and white, cobble beaches are washed by the blue-green waters of one of Ontario's most beautiful large lakes.

It is a busy place on a summer day and you'll meet vacationing campers who are not normally hikers, but who have walked from the Cyprus Lake campground to see the natural wonders. The tiny, picturesque Indian Head Cove is also a favourite rest spot for the many divers who frequent this coastline.

The trail is short but you will need two to three hours to explore it properly. Scrambling over rocks and boulder beaches also slows the pace.

If you are not camping in the park you should check with the park office before driving through to the Head of Trails where there is parking. The park office will provide a map and directions. There is no charge.

From the parking lot, look for a sign pointing to Head of Trails. From here, take the trail that leads to Marr Lake. The walking is easy at first due to the chipwood path and boardwalks. It becomes a little more challenging as it climbs. It then descends over a very rocky path that appears to be an old stream bed, emerging onto the shore of tiny Marr Lake where the path becomes quite marshy.

Marr Lake appears to be a landlocked cove of Georgian Bay. At it's far end, a large wall of smooth, white rubble beach separates it from its parent. It is very pretty and relatively quiet compared to the Georgian Bay waterfront you will soon visit.

The path travels around Marr Lake in a northwesterly direction until it ends on the rubble beach. Here you will have your first view of Georgian Bay. There are interpretive signs on the beach.

Cross the beach, making for the cliffs to your right. It's a challenging walk because the small boulders that form the beach shift and move as you walk over them, so that your feet slide backwards. These boulders become quite large as you near the cliff. You will want to find a spot to sit here so that you can admire the view. The first headland you come to is a fine viewpoint, but is often claimed by early-bird hikers. If you climb down below it just to the right you can get an interesting view of the Grotto, an enormous cave that looks just perfect for a pirate's hideaway. There are at least two underwater entrances to the Grotto from Georgian Bay. This is not the best view, but does give a different perspective.

Retrace your steps and climb upward to the top of the escarpment following the red or white blazes on rocks or tree trunks. There are stupendous views. Offshore you can see Bear's Rump Island as well as Flowerpot Island and the curve of the large boulder beach.

Look for a white double blaze on a tree to your left which leads onto an overhang opposite the Grotto.

The big cave is awesome and majestic. Below you, swallows fly in and out of the huge cave mouth and clear, shallow water rolls endlessly in and out. You can climb down and enter the cave to explore it but it's a challenging climb back up. **You should exercise caution all along this stretch of coastline where there have been some fatal accidents**.

The Natural Arch is a few metres farther along the trail. This is a huge cavernous opening in the rock and you stand on the edge and look down into a small pool. At the outer rim a large hole is open to Georgian Bay offering a glimpse of blue water.

Continuing on, the next point of interest is Indian Head Cove, a tiny, breathtakingly lovely bay surrounded by high cliffs. Its white cobble beach is a favourite spot of divers who sun themselves between plunges into the cool blue-green depths of Georgian Bay. This is a lovely lunch spot if you can find a place to sit.

The trail skirts the cliffs around the cove and continues along the edge of the escarpment to Halfway Rock Point. This is another pretty bay with a boulder beach. A couple of interpretive signs erected by the park provide some facts about the area. For example, the escarpment face you can see to the east rises some 30 m. However, it also plunges into the water for another 170 m. Just beyond this spot is the deepest part of Georgian Bay.

From this beach you have a choice of turning inland and walking down the west side of Horse Lake to return to the Head of Trails, or you can continue another 250 m or so along the Georgian Bay shoreline and take the trail down the east side of Horse Lake to the Head of Trails.

The walk down the west side is easy, and is recommended as the trail for children, or less experienced hikers, as it follows boardwalks for most of the way. There is an interpretive station at the head of Horse Lake which explains the dynamics of a disappearing watercourse.

Soon the trail joins up with the Marr Lake Trail, crosses a pretty set of rapids between Horse and Cyprus lakes and returns you to the Head of Trails.

Lion's Head Loop

Bruce Trail

- **LENGTH:** 18 km (6+ hours)
- **DEGREE OF DIFFICULTY:** Moderate to challenging
- **TYPE OF TRAIL:** Loop
- **LOCATION:** Lion's Head, Bruce Peninsula

HOW TO GET THERE:

Although hikers sometimes find spots to park their cars close to the start of the trail, these are actually private parking areas belonging to local cottagers. It is recommended that hikers park their cars in the schoolyard on Moore Street, just off Main Street.

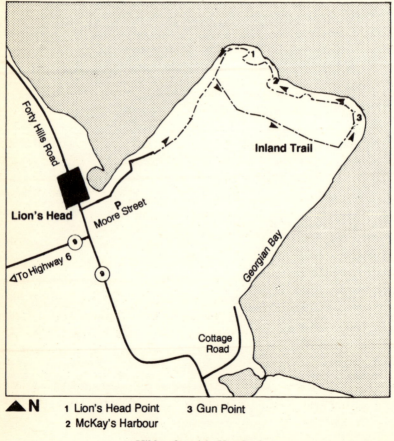

N

1 Lion's Head Point   3 Gun Point
2 McKay's Harbour

Hiking Ontario's Heartland

From the schoolyard, continue down Moore Street for 1.3 km until you come to a STOP sign and private road sign. Look to your right for the white blaze that signifies the Bruce Trail. Follow the white blazes. **Not recommended for small children**.

• • •

This is an absolutely spectacular hike offering views that cannot be surpassed anywhere in the world. Naturally, there's a catch. You should do this hike only when the weather is good, as it can be hazardous in inclement weather. About 1 km of the trail traverses the high cliffs of the Niagara Escarpment and at times you will walk only inches from the edge where a slip can mean certain death. There are no guardrails and it is not for the fainthearted. Bad weather can also affect water levels on the beach at McKay's Harbour, making it dangerous or impassable.

On a good day, however, when the sun makes Georgian Bay a splendid expanse of blue, the rewards of this hike are fantastic. The trail leads completely around two sides and part of a third side of the peninsula known as Lion's Head on the Bruce Peninsula. If the day is bright you'll be stunned by the beauty of the turquoise waters of Georgian Bay that lap the rocky shoreline many metres below the cliff edge. To the south you can see the green-capped white cliffs of Cape Dundas and Barrier Island. To the north the cliffs of White Bluff, Cape Chin and Cabot Head spear into this beautiful lake.

At the start of the trail there is a curious chimney-shaped hollow rock chamber that you can enter through a hole in the side. Also, if you look carefully in the forest you may see orchids.

Not bad for one trail!

The loop starts in the village of Lion's Head, travels about 3 km up the side of Isthmus Bay on the north shore of this point of land, then cuts across country to emerge on the south side just west of Gun Point. It then follows the edge of the escarpment north to McKay's Harbour, drops down to the beach, climbs back up again to Lion's Head Point and travels back down the side of Isthmus Bay to return to the village.

Leaving the parking area, follow white blazes along a gravel road and past a couple of boulders strategically placed to stop cars from entering. The path winds at first through an evergreen forest, rising gently as the forest changes to a mixed bush. The gravel road makes a turn to the right but the trail continues in a straight line and narrows. The path now enters an attractive forested area of rock outcroppings, thickly carpeted with bracken fern.

You will come to the chimney rock very quickly so keep your eyes open for the double blaze that the Bruce Trail Club uses to signify a trail attraction or turn. The entrance hole is located in a cliff to your right.

From here the trail ascends steadily, crossing a very rocky area until you come to the first lookout over Isthmus Bay. You'll be stopped in your tracks, the view is so stunning. You'll see across the bay to White Bluff and below your feet to the rocks shimmering beneath the turquoise of the lake.

From now on until you branch off on the inland stretch of the trail, about 1 km from here, you will follow the edge of the escarpment, catching tantalizing glimpses of Isthmus Bay. Each lookout is marked with a double blue blaze to ensure you won't miss one.

The turn-off to the inland trail is very well marked, thanks to members of the Bruce Trail Club. The trail turns sharply to the left into the forest, following blue blazes on the trees for about 4 km. The path is narrow and overgrown, and pungent with wild leeks. Look almost immediately for the round-leaved orchis, a tall white stem of tiny orchids with two huge, leathery-green leaves lying flat to the ground.

In about 2 km you will come to a fork in the trail where there are a couple of well-executed signs, one pointing to McKay's Harbour (yellow blaze), the other (blue blaze) to Barrow Bay. Follow the Barrow Bay path. After a short time the path becomes confusing so make sure you are following the blue blazes.

About 1 km farther on you will come out onto an old logging road. Turn left and follow the road about 500 m. This road diminishes into a very overgrown path. This eventually leads to an area of flat rocky pavement where poison ivy runs rampant. You will encounter this plant on numerous occasions for most of the rest of the walk.

In fact soon, when you emerge onto the southern edge of the

escarpment, you may wonder which is worse—going over the edge or tippytoeing through the poison ivy, which flourishes on the path near the inner walls of the cliff.

When you leave the inland trail where it meets the main Bruce Trail, turn left following the white blazes. This trail hugs the cliff, its proximity to the edge at times making strong men weak at the knees. There are stupendous views over this great expanse of blue water.

The trail passes the dramatic rockface known as Gun Point, turns northwards and winds between cedars and open, flat terraces overlooking the water for about 1 km. It turns inland slightly and switchbacks up and down until it reaches a blue marker that signifies a lookout point a few steps downhill. Back on the trail, continue through the bush until you see a yellow marker (which leads back through the bush to the inland trail). Turn sharply to the right, still following the white blazes and descend a series of steep hills to McKay's Harbour.

You will now have been walking almost 4 hours. There is a small sandy beach and lots of flat rocks so this is a good lunch spot. Its also a perfect spot to pull off the boots and cool off the feet.

To continue on the trail, follow the line of the beach northwards and turn inland onto a rocky plateau where the beach ends. Lots of poison ivy here, too.

The trail enters the forest again and starts to climb the escarpment, passing underneath an enormous rock overhang. The trail continues to climb for about 2 km to the top of the escarpment, again offering marvellous views until you reach Lion's Head Lookout. This is an impressive flat-topped cliff that the more daring sometimes rappel down.

The trail climbs a couple of steep hills then reaches the point where it intersects once again with the inland trail which you took to strike across country earlier in the hike. You are now on familiar ground as you retrace your steps through the forest and past the chimney-shaped rock formation towards the village of Lion's Head.

Osler Bluffs

Bruce Trail

- **LENGTH**: 12 km (4 hours)
- **DEGREE OF DIFFICULTY**: Moderate to challenging
- **TYPE OF TRAIL**: Loop • **LOCATION**: Collingwood

HOW TO GET THERE:

Take Highway 24 and turn west onto Poplar Sideroad at Nottawa. Follow Poplar Sideroad to the end and turn right for about .5 km, then turn left onto Grey Road 19. Look for blue arrows. Park on the grass shoulder at top of hill on right.

• • •

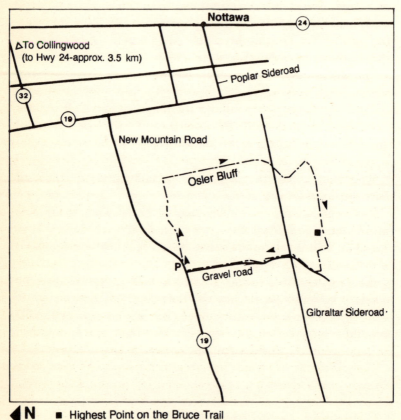

N ■ Highest Point on the Bruce Trail

This trail is worth the time and effort involved if only to tell your friends you have hiked to the highest point of the entire Bruce Trail. For statistic lovers, it's 540 m above sea level.

But that's icing on the cake. The real payoff comes from marvellous views from the top of Osler Bluff, a towering three-sided promontory on the famed Niagara Escarpment. From its pinnacle the eye takes in the patchwork quilt of the valley directly below, and beyond it the blue waters of Georgian Bay stretching to the horizon. The many hills of the escarpment roll away to the east, and to the northwest are the Blue Mountains of the Collingwood area.

If this weren't enough, you can feast your eyes on unusual ferns and acres of wildflowers such as the shy jack-in-the-pulpit, dainty columbine, blue phlox, false Solomon's seal and the sparkling spears of white baneberry. All this is guarded over by what appeared to this hiker to be Ontario's largest toad!

Osler Bluff is named for a prominent 19th-century Toronto lawyer, Britton Bath Osler, who built an elegant 15-room home known as The Castle, on top of the bluff. It is now in ruins.

The trail is well marked with the familiar diamond-shaped blaze of the Bruce Trail Association, and a blue blaze, which signifies that a side trail has been opened up to provide a looped route.

Ascent of the bluff can be achieved through some rugged rockclimbing, or via the more gentle, though still steep, slopes of Osler Bluffs Ski Club.

Ater parking your car on the wide grass shoulder on the west side of Grey Road 19, cross the road to access the trail from a farm lane. The trail is marked by a blue blaze. Follow the track about 500 m until it narrows and becomes a grassy trail fringed by heavy bush. Soon you will come to a lookout with a view over rolling meadows to Georgian Bay. At this point, the trail turns sharply to the right into the bushes, eventually leading into a very marshy area. As you pick your way through the marsh watch carefully; the trail veers off to the right and is easy to lose.

The trail continues gently upwards until it enters an overgrown meadow where there is a reservoir used for snowmaking by the ski resort. Good views to the north over the Bay.

If you wish to scale the bluff face to ascend to the upper trail you must access it from a path running on the south side of the reservoir. Be warned, this is a steep and dangerous climb. There is a black, rubberized wire handrail of sorts to assist in climbing.

The recommended approach is to walk to the far side of the reservoir, turn left along its upper end and take the wide path up the Osler Bluff ski run. It's a long pull, but easily done with a couple of rest stops. This long, wide hill turns to the left near the top. Just below the summit on your right looms a huge cliff face. The Bruce Trail turns a sharp right at the top of this rock, but first continue past it a short way and follow the ski hill to a lookout on your left. Now the views are starting to be worth the climb. The ski resort communities stretch out below and you can see the wide sweep of Nottawasaga Bay.

Regaining the trail, follow it until it forks. Take the right fork which leads to the western edge of the bluff. You are now at the top of the rockface that is climbed by means of the wire rope and you can congratulate yourself for either being smart enough to avoid it, or for actually scaling it and arriving at this point intact.

The views from here offer a different perspective. You can see Grey Road 19 where you parked your car, and beyond that the ridges that culminate in the Blue Mountains.

The trail now veers to the left and into the forest high above the surrounding countryside. Ignore the next fork you come to and keep straight ahead. A little farther on there is another fork where, if you take the path that goes off to the right, it will lead you back to the car if you want to cut short the trip. You will now have been hiking for about 30 minutes.

Continuing on, the trail runs alongside a laneway, which is used by traffic accessing ski chalets. The trail eventually emerges onto the laneway and follows it for a short distance to a locked gate. Through the gate, the laneway continues at the edge of a high meadow and ends at a T-junction. Turn left onto this country road and walk for about 1 km. When you reach the point where a steep hill goes downwards and there is a wide grass shoulder on your right, look beyond the grass shoulder for the trail opening into the trees. Just inside the trees the trail runs by an enormous and mysterious deep, dark cleft in the ground.

This area is characteristic of the escarpment. Long, narrow

clefts split the ground here and there, and huge, moss-covered rocks lie scattered, ferns spilling from fissures. You are now at the top of Osler Bluff and a few short climbs will bring you to the edge of the escarpment. Two rocky ledges, high over the surrounding countryside, offer good lunch spots.

High as you are, you are not yet at the highest point of the Bruce Trail. To get there, continue on the trail as it winds around the eastern rim—and often to the very edge—of the bluffs. Where the trail forks, take the right trail deeper into the forest away from the cliff edge. The air is redolent with the smell of wild leeks. It is so lush here it is reminiscent of a western rainforest.

In another 500 m or so the trail splits again. To the right is the main Bruce Trail, and to the left is the side trail to the highest point. The trail climbs steadily but gently. About 15 minutes along, watch for the double blaze that signifies a turn. Turn left, then up a steep hill, following blue trail markers. This will lead you to a fence line. Squeeze through and you will find yourself in a meadow. This is the highest point in the entire 773-km length of the Bruce Trail.

Retrace your steps back to the fence and follow blue blazes to your right. The trail now starts to descend. When you reach a junction, turn off to the right, still following blue blazes. A gravel path leads alongside an open field with Provincial Park signs posted. Halfway up the hill, look for a Bruce Trail sign off to your left and follow the trail across a field and into a forest. The trail winds through the forest and rejoins the gravel road at a cross-roads.

Stay on the gravel road and follow it down a long steep hill that has a bend in it. At the bottom of this hill you will see a double blue blaze for a turn to your right. This side trail takes you through the Petun Conservation Area, climbing up a lovely, leafy, rocky escarpment area and descending across a long boardwalk over a bog. After crossing a stream you will pass an old camp building and shortly afterwards a gate will provide an exit on to the road. Turn right and follow the gravel road about 1 km to your car.

The Near North

REGIONAL OVERVIEW

THOSE NOT fortunate enough to live in Ontario's Near North call this area their vacationland. Majestic forests, small sparkling lakes, Algonquin Park and the Almaguin Highlands, Georgian Bay, Manitoulin Island and the wondrous beauty of the North Channel. The superlatives never end, nor do the attractions of this superb area of Ontario.

The Near North's major trail is undoubtedly the sections of the **Voyageur Trail** that traverse this area. The Voyageur could vie with any trail anywhere for beauty and ruggedness. It is a trail still in the making. Begun in 1974, volunteers are completing it section by section. Plans are for the trail to be a continuous 1,100-km hiking trail across Northern Ontario, from South Baymouth on Manitoulin Island west to Thunder Bay. Eventually, an eastward extension will follow the route of the French and Mattawa Rivers, while a westward extension will run to the Manitoba border.

Several sections have already been completed. These include a section from Iron Bridge west to Sault Ste. Marie, and one through Lake Superior Provincial Park that takes in the dramatic scenery of the Lake Superior coastline. A third section travels through the wilderness of Pukaskwa National Park, and a fourth along the Lake Superior coast in the Terrace Bay area.

Some sections of the trail travel through unbelievably remote country. Anyone planning to hike these should first contact the trail association to ascertain trail conditions. You will find the members very helpful. The Voyageur is a trail for serious hikers so you should have maps and a compass, and know how to use them. You should also never, ever, enter these sections of the trail without leaving details of your plans and itinerary with a responsible adult.

Provincial parks in the Near North offer good hiking opportunities. One is **Halfway Lake Provincial Park** located on Highway 144, about 90 km northwest of Sudbury, with four trails. They include a short nature trail, a 7.5-km hike and a 30-km backpacking trail that all leave from the main campground area. A fourth, of approximately 15 km, is at the northern end of the park on the east side of the highway. Trail maps are available from the park. The 7.5-km trail includes a visit to a lookout tower for absolutely splendid views of rolling forested country and lakes. There are lots of opportunities to view moose in this park, as well as some interesting rock outcroppings and a variety of huge, multicoloured mushrooms.

In the northeast, **Driftwood Provincial Park**, situated on the shores of the mighty Ottawa River, has 12 km of trails. The hiker can explore wetlands, forest, high eskers and rocky ridges. From lookouts above the Ottawa River you can see the Province of Quebec's Gatineau Hills. A few kilometres east of here, on Highway 17 at Chalk River, the **Petawawa National Forestry Institute** also offers short walking trails. For more information from the Institute telephone (613) 589-2880.

There is an interesting network of trails on 304 ha at North Bay's **Canadore College**. These range from short walks through scenic wooded areas to longer hikes to high ground from where there are views of the Manitou Islands in Lake Nipissing. You can continue walking to the top of Duchesnay Falls. The trails are accessible from Highway 17 west of the city, or call the local travel association at (705) 474-6634.

At Sudbury, there are good trails in the **Lake Laurentian Conservation Area**. Trails range from a short birdwatching trail to a 15-km hiking trail that circles Lake Laurentian. Some trails lead around a marsh that is a good spot for waterfowl viewing. The blueberry bushes are amazing. More information from the Nickel District Conservation Authority is available by calling (705) 674-5249.

About 40 km north of Parry Sound, **The Shawanaga Trail** starts from the Pointe Au Baril Community Centre on Highway 69. This moderately rugged trail over Precambrian Shield country runs east for 10 km to Wilson Lake, then south for 6 km to Wilson Lake Road. It travels the route of an old Department of Lands and Forests telephone line that linked fire towers to headquarters in Parry Sound. A southern access point can be found 2 km north of the Shawanaga River at Wilson Lake Road on Highway 69. Obtain more information from the Parry Sound District Office of the Ministry of Natural Resources at (705) 746-4201.

South of here on Highway 69, north of Victoria Harbour, the **McRae Lake–Gibson River Wilderness Area** offers a 22-km loop on Crown land. This route circles around McRae Lake, east of the highway, passing a number of small lakes, some of which are excellent for swimming. The trail winds through the southern edge of Precambrian Shield country, with excellent views. Access this trail from Highway 69 and Georgian Bay Road, approximately 3 km north of Six Mile Lake Provincial Park. More information is available from the Bracebridge Area Office, Ministry of Natural Resources at (705) 645-8747.

To the west, in the Muskoka–Haliburton area there are 14.5 km of trails at the **Bracebridge Resource Management Centre** on the east side of Highway 11, just north of Bracebridge. These trails run through a forest area operated by the Ministry of Natural Resources. More information is available from the Bracebridge Area Office.

Farther west still, are 27 km of trails at the **Leslie M. Frost Natural Resources Centre**, an outdoors educational facility operated by the Ministry of Natural Resources. Trails are on Precambrian Shield country, through lovely hardwood and white pine forests, around St. Nora Lake. There is also a lookout tower. The Leslie M. Frost Centre is located on the east side of Highway 35, approximately 15 km south of Dorset.

There are a growing number of tourist outfitters now offering guided hiking holidays in many regions of Ontario. In this area is one that offers hiking packages in Kawagama Lake near Dorset, and on Crown lands in the Haliburton area. Others offer packages in Algonquin. More information is available from the Ministry of Culture, Tourism and Recreation, which produces the *Ontario Adventure Guide,* a catalogue of outdoor holidays. Refer to the address in the Appendix.

Trails of Algonquin Provincial Park

- **LENGTH:** 1.5 to 88 km (1 hour to several days)
- **DEGREE OF DIFFICULTY:** Easy to very challenging
- **TYPE OF TRAIL:** Loops
- **LOCATION:** Algonquin Provincial Park, Whitney

HOW TO GET THERE:

Trails are accessed from a variety of locations. Most short, day hikes are accessible from Highway 60 which runs east to west through the southern portion of Algonquin Provincial Park, 45 km east of Huntsville. Two on the east side of the park are accessible from north of Pembroke. One goes south into the park from Deux Rivieres. Two long-distance backpacking trails are accessed from

▲N □ Major day trails and two backpacking trails accessed from Highway 60.

The Near North

151

Highway 60. One of these, the Western Uplands Trail is also accessible from Rain Lake, approximately 27 km east of the village of Kearney.

• • •

Algonquin! The name evokes visions of tramping through conifer woods, of glimpsing a moose lifting its dripping head from the shallows of a lake, of long climbs to lookouts for views of rolling hills ablaze with flaming fall colours. Algonquin is all of these, and more, much more.

This 7,600-km² provincial park, created in 1893, embraces thousands of hectares of forests, lakes, rivers and streams. To really know its soul, you must hike or canoe away from the main Highway 60 corridor into its heart. Only then can you start to discover its mysteries.

In Algonquin the hiker can choose from 13 trails that fan out from the Highway 60 corridor, as well as two trails entering from the park's remote eastern section, another one from the north, and two long-distance backpacking trails for experienced hikers only.

The longest of the trails leading from Highway 60 are the **Mizzy Lake**, the **Track and Tower** (covered elsewhere in this book) and the new **Centennial Ridges** trails. These take from 4 to 6 hours each to complete.

The 11-km Mizzy Lake trail is accessed from the north side of Highway 60, 15 km west of the West Gate and just past the road into Arrowhon Pines Lodge. It visits nine small lakes and ponds to provide opportunities for wildlife viewing. If you can be at

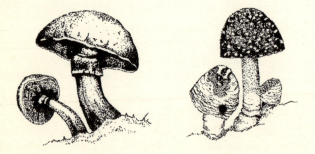

particular points of the trail at prime viewing times the chances are good for spotting moose and other wildlife. Part of the trail follows the bed of the old, abandoned Ottawa, Arnprior and Parry Sound Railway. At one time, a train went through this area every 20 minutes.

A 2-km side trail at roughly the halfway point leads along an old logging road to a point where there are some "bear's nests." These are manufactured unintentially by black bears, not to sleep in, but as a by-product of the bear's reaching for nuts. The nests are formed when branches break off and lodge in a tree crotch where the bear has been sitting and reaching for beechnuts.

Hikers can return to Highway 60 via either the Arrowhon Road or the Weldwood Road, rather than by the trail, if desired. As with the other Algonquin trails, there is an excellent trail guide booklet available for the Mizzy Lake Trail, and this may be purchased, or borrowed, from the trail start.

The Centennial Ridges Trail is a rugged, 10-km loop named to celebrate the park's centennial year in 1993. The trail follows two high parallel ridges east of Whitefish Lake offering some of the most outstanding cliff-top viewpoints in the park. The trail pays tribute to some of the famous personalities associated with the park during its 100-year history. A trail guide booklet may be picked up at the start of the trail, which is 37.6 km east of the main West Gate entrance on Highway 60, and about 2 km west of the entrance to the Rock Lake Campground.

Although quite short, the 1.9-km **Lookout Trail** that starts 39.7 km east of the West Gate, offers a steep and rugged climb to the top of a cliff for some stunning Algonquin views. From this lookout you can see Lake of Two Rivers, Kearney Lake and Little Rock Lake, as well as the forested Algonquin uplands that seem to stretch to infinity. The trail guide booklet explores the geology of Algonquin and explains how these rocks and cliffs came to be here.

Also worth a look is the 5.1-km **Booth's Rock Trail** that explores a cliff top beyond the Rock Lake Campground, one of the few car-camping grounds in the park that is not close to the main highway. From the top of Booth's Rock there are magnificent views of Rock and Whitefish lakes and several hundred kilometres of Algonquin's forested and rolling terrain. The trail is named for

J.R. Booth, one of Canada's most famous lumber barons, whose railroad cut through the park in the last century. The trail follows part of the old railbed and passes through a rockcut that was dynamited for the railroad. It also skims the edge of the old Barclay Estate on Rock Lake that once was owned by Judge George Barclay, a cousin of J.R. Booth.

Other short walking trails in the Highway 60 corridor explore a spruce bog, a beaver pond, rapids on the Oxtongue River and various lake and forest ecosystems.

On the east side of the park are the **Achray Trail System** and the shorter, but very dramatic **Barron Canyon Trail**. These trails are not readily accessible to the weekend visitor to the park's Highway 60 corridor, the closest being at least a 6-hour return drive.

The trails are accessed by following the Highway 17 bypass 3.5 km west of Forest Lea Road, (about 9 km west of Pembroke) then turning south onto County Road 26. Drive 300 m then turn right at the Achray Road and drive 26 km on this logging road that enters the eastern portion of Algonquin Park at Sand Lake Gate. The turnoff to the Achray campground is another 19.2 km, some 8 km past the entrance to the Barron Canyon Trail. You can camp at the Achray Campground, 50 km from Pembroke, and tackle the trails from there.

The 1.5-km Barron Canyon Trail is not really a hike, but it is so spectacular that you cannot stay at the Achray Campground without visiting it. The trail leads to the canyon rim, 100 m above the Barron River, which flows through the canyon on its way to join the Ottawa River. From roughly the 1830s to the 1930s, the canyon was the scene of log drives every spring, when thousands of red and white pine logs were driven down the swollen river.

The canyon was caused by a fault in the earth's surface, exposing minerals rarely seen in Algonquin. This results in some rare plants growing on the canyon walls. A number of species of birds nest here. In winter, bald and golden eagles visit to feed on carrion left by wolves which have killed deer trapped on the frozen waters of the river.

The Achray Trail System offers a system of loops of varying short lengths, to which can be added a linear hike for a total of 15 km.

The loops lead from the campground around tiny Berm Lake and Johnston Lake. A linear trail starts here and leads to a panoramic lookout and finally to the scenic High Falls between Stratton Lake and High Falls Lake. The trails offer an excellent opportunity for walks through the pine forests of the park's remote interior.

The **Brent Crater Trail** is the only one accessed from the park's northern perimeter and this is reached by about 32 km of rough road from the tiny village of Deux Riviere on Highway 17, the Trans-Canada Highway. This short, 2-km walk explores the 3 km-wide crater believed to have been formed some 450 million years ago when a meteorite crashed into the earth. The crater has been the subject of much scientific study since it is one of only 100 known fossil meteorite craters in the world, and one of the best preserved.

If you are ready for the really big challenge, Algonquin provides two remote backpacking trails. On the park's west side, in its mountainous western highlands is the aptly named **Western Uplands Trail**. This is an extremely rugged trail that should not be tackled by beginners, unless accompanied by an experienced trail guide. It consists of a series of loops ranging from 32 km to 88 km on hilly terrain over rocky ridges, around lakes and through bogs. Good boots and equipment are essential for a comfortable trip. Hikers tackling the long-distance trails need to obtain an interior camping permit from the park, for which there is a daily charge. It is wise to book ahead because of the popularity of the sites. Park staff issue a limited number of permits each day for each access point so that hikers can have a quality "away from it all" experience. This also ensures that sufficient campsite facilities are available for those on the trail.

Access is from either Highway 60, 3 km east of the West Gate, or from the trail's northernmost end at the Rain Lake Access Point.

Algonquin's other remote trail is the **Highland Trail**, which travels south of Highway 60 from a parking lot located just west of the Mew Lake Campground, 29.7 km east of the West Gate. This trail offers two loops, 19 km and 35 km, and the shortest makes a good day hike provided you do it when the daylight hours are longest.

Again, there is a daily quota of hikers allowed on the trail and permits are needed. The shortest loop traverses the shoreline of

Provoking Lake and loops back to the trail start. The longer trail provides a challenging hike of three days if you are to do it comfortably and give yourself time to experience the park's interior and enjoy its remote lakes.

Both the Highland Trail and the Western Uplands Trail offer primitive campsites. Hikers are allowed to camp on the Provoking Lake sites for only one night during most of the summer to ensure sites are available for newcomers.

A trail map is available from the park and you should have this before tackling these long-distance hikes. Reservations may be made by calling the park at (705) 633-5538, or through the Ministry of Natural Resources at the address given in the Appendix.

Track and Tower Trail

Algonquin Provincial Park

- **LENGTH:** 9 km (4 hours) • **DEGREE OF DIFFICULTY:** Moderate
- **TYPE OF TRAIL:** Loop
- **LOCATION:** Algonquin Provincial Park, Whitney

HOW TO GET THERE:

Take Highway 60 to Algonquin Provincial Park. The trail starts from a parking lot on the south side of Highway 60, 25 km east of the main West Gate entrance. If travelling west from Whitney, the parking lot is just west of the Mew Lake Campground.

• • •

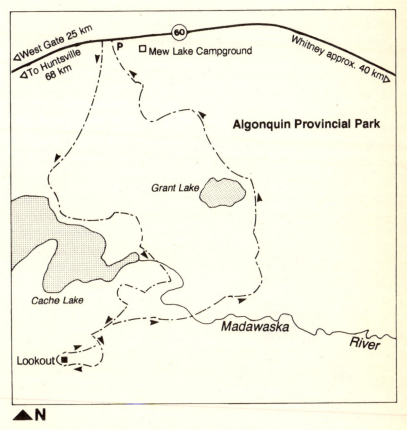

lines another shortcut back to the parking lot. To continue on to the lookout, take the path to the right. You will almost immediately start climbing through a hardwood bush. At the top of the incline there is an enormous crag that stretches for some 100 m. The path travels along its base to a set of many wooden steps leading up the cliff face. Arrows point the way to the fire tower site. There is nothing there but moose scat now. However, continue past and in a few minutes you will emerge from the bush onto a flat wide plateau overlooking some of Algonquin's finest scenery. Cache Lake lies below and the forested Algonquin Highlands stretch to the west and north.

You are now at the half-way point of the trail. The return trip is made via the wooden steps and down the incline until you come to an arrow pointing off to the right. From here the path joins the old railbed that curves beneath a high rocky outcrop festooned with lush greenery. (The park guide booklet shows a picture of this spot taken around 1900. In it, the rail lines are shown snaking around a denuded cliff. There is no vegetation other than a little coarse grass.)

The evidence of an old 15-m-high trestle bridge over the Madawaska is still here in the bridge abutments. You will marvel at the challenges faced by the men who built this structure so long ago. The trail crosses the river by a new footbridge and turns right, continuing along the tracks. Fresh moose scat and some gnawed branches are evidence of a recent visit by this huge Algonquin resident.

After leaving the tracks, the path continues into the forest until it reaches tiny Grant Lake. The path goes past the lake and meanders through the woods for perhaps another 4 km before emerging at the east end of the parking lot.

Etienne Trail System

Samuel de Champlain Provincial Park

- **LENGTH:** 9 km (4 to 5 hours)
- **DEGREE OF DIFFICULTY:** Moderate to challenging
- **TYPE OF TRAIL:** Loop • **LOCATION:** Mattawa

HOW TO GET THERE:

The park entrance is on the Trans-Canada Highway (Highway 17) 14 km west of Mattawa, 52 km east of North Bay. The park operates mid-May to the end of September. There is a day-use fee during the operating season. Park trails may be used during the non-operating season but no facilities are provided and hikers

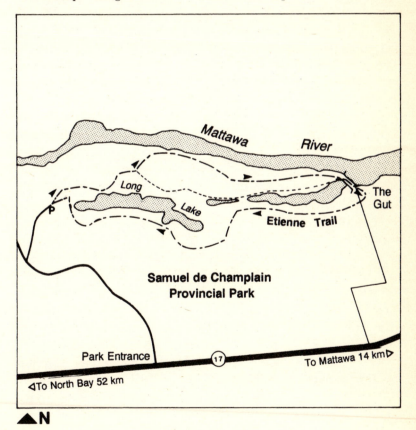

are cautioned to pay strict attention to trail signs for their safety.

• • •

The Etienne Trail System offers four delightful hikes that interconnect, three of which traverse the high cliffs along the scenic and historic Mattawa River. They explore the ecological, geological, natural, and historical aspects of the park. A guide booklet is available from the park office. None of the trails are long, but they are time-consuming because of rugged walking conditions and the amount of ridge climbing involved. There is also a great temptation to stop over-long to admire the scenery, and to reflect on the historic associations of this lovely river with the opening up of this country.

The guidebook tells us that about 12,000 years ago, a very much larger Mattawa River was the main drainage outlet of the Great Lakes. This lasted about 5,000 years. Then, as the huge ice-cap that covered most of the land retreated, the northern lands rose and cut off the Mattawa flow, leaving us with the river we see today.

The name, Mattawa, is believed to be of Algonkian origin, meaning "meeting of the waters." It refers to the confluence of the Mattawa with the mighty Ottawa River a few kilometres downstream from the park.

The river was part of the great water route between Montreal and the west and was travelled by the major explorers, including Samuel de Champlain and Etienne Brûlé. Brûlé, in 1610, was the first white person to see the valley. At that time the area was a hunting ground of the Nipissing tribe of the Algonkians. For the next 200 years, the river was travelled by voyageurs and missionaries, and by coureurs de bois who risked death at the hands of the Iroquois to transport furs. In the 1760s, when the fur trade was at its height, it was nothing for 50 huge canoes to round the bend and paddle past the cliffs that today are used as scenic lookouts. Following a merge between the two great trading companies, the Hudson Bay Company and the North West Company in 1821, the route was changed. It was cheaper and quicker to transport goods by way of Hudson Bay and the Mattawa became a quiet, peaceful river again.

There is no evidence that either Champlain or Brûlé ever landed in the vicinity of the park, and there are few good landing places along the steep and thickly forested river banks. On the other hand, there is no evidence to prove that they did not land either. Walking the trail it is easy to picture the days when daring voyageurs paddled birchbark canoes along this waterway, wondering what dangers and discomforts awaited them as they explored this harsh yet beautiful continent.

The Historical Trail, marked by a blue arrow, is the park's longest, and reminders of the past appear as soon as you start the hike. The path leads over small boulders that once formed the bed of the ancient large river. As the trail starts to climb, the cries of a crested flycatcher and some small warblers echo through the forest. After about 15 minutes the trail rises steeply, necessitating some boulder jumping over a solid mass of rock. At the top you will stand on the park's highest point south of the Mattawa, some 250 m above sea level. Below the cliff to your left is tiny Long Lake, glistening prettily in the sunlight.

The path travels close to the cliff edge for about 50 m and then turns northward and goes down the other side of the ridge. At the top of the next ridge white arrows lead to a lookout over Moore Lake Beach on the Amable du Fond River which starts in Algonquin Provincial Park and joins the Mattawa here.

The main trail continues over typical Canadian Shield terrain, which means there are lots of rocky outcrops and ridges to climb, and marvellous views of rolling forested hills stretching to infinity. The park trail guide booklet indicates we are walking over a still-active fault in the earth's crust and that the area experiences minor tremors each year.

All the Etienne trails follow the same path for roughly the first 1 km, so be sure to follow the blue arrow when the trails diverge. The blue trail continues through mixed bush, up and over steep ridges. Blueberries grow in profusion so in season you can pretend you are picking some on the way up while catching a breath. Numerous burned stumps tell the story of past forest fires. To the far left you catch your first glimpse of the Mattawa far below and the high forested cliffs of its northern shoreline.

The path continues downhill and in about 10 minutes you will arrive at the first lookout over the river. The view is breathtaking. The river lies some 200 m below, and it is wide, placid and beautiful with lofty cliffs crowned with white pines on either side. You will now have been walking roughly 1 hour.

The trail continues close to the cliff edge for some 300 m, where deer scat is plentiful on the rocky ground. Trees and ferns cling for dear life to the cliff sides, and the high shores across the river are a mirror image of the ones the trail passes over.

Heading south, away from the river, the trail passes through woods with a fairly open canopy, encouraging lots of new growth that threatens to take over the path in places. Walking is fairly easy for a while over the soft forest floor. Small patches of what appears to be reindeer moss are an interesting diversion.

After about 500 m the trail crosses a small swamp by means of logs, climbs a small rocky ridge and re-emerges onto the cliffs overlooking the river.

The path again traces the cliff top for about 1.5 km, climbing and descending rocky ridges and keeping the river in sight. The view broadens to include longer reaches of the river as you approach the eastern-most point. So pervasive is the history of this place it would come as no surprise if a freighter canoe loaded with coureur de bois came around the bend.

When you reach the eastern-most point, the path turns southward and crosses a high wooden bridge over The Gut, an inlet of the river lined by rocky canyon walls. On the other side of the bridge there is easy access to the shoreline and this makes a good lunch stop where you can enjoy a long view of the Mattawa as it journeys eastward to join the Ottawa River.

From the beach, the trail climbs up a long ridge and merges with another trail. Near the top of the ridge are massive boulders that were carried, mounded and left by glacial ice, as if a giant child had used them to play with and tossed them carelessly aside. The trail squeezes through a small, narrow chasm and starts a long, steady climb, leaving the river. It runs high above The Gut and follows the cliff edge for about 2 km over a variety of terrain, from rocky outcrops covered with lichens to swampy areas around beaver ponds decorated with jewelweed, Joe pye-weed and spearmint. There's some tricky walking as you pass the second beaver pond and you will notice you are very close to the edge of the cliff with a sheer drop to The Gut.

After crossing what appears to be a dry, rocky streambed, the trail continues over rocky outcroppings and crosses a high ridge before entering a shady pine forest. From here, the trail crosses a series of ridges until you come to the low ground at the end of The Gut. Climbing again, the trail crosses another series of ridges through a forested area for about 2 km, skirts a beaver pond, crosses a wet spot and emerges on the south side of Long Lake.

From the shoreline you will climb what seems to be a never-ending hill but at the top there is a bench where you can sit and look out over the tops of the pines.

The trail continues in an up and down fashion for about 1 km, then comes to a long boardwalk over a spruce bog. After crossing a bridge over the end of Long Lake turn left onto the park road and it is a short walk back to the parking lot.

Trails of Killarney Provincial Park

- **LENGTH:** 2 to 100 km (1 hour to several days)
- **DEGREE OF DIFFICULTY:** Easy to very challenging
- **TYPE OF TRAIL:** Loop and linear • **LOCATION:** Killarney

HOW TO GET THERE:

From Highway 69, approximately 35 km south of Sudbury, turn west onto Secondary Road 637 and travel 65 km to the park.

• • •

Killarney Provincial Park is one of those places that needs no introduction to the Ontario outdoors crowd. People speak of it with awe and visit year after year to renew its acquaintance, often making reservations at the provincial park and nearby lodges a year in advance to avoid disappointment.

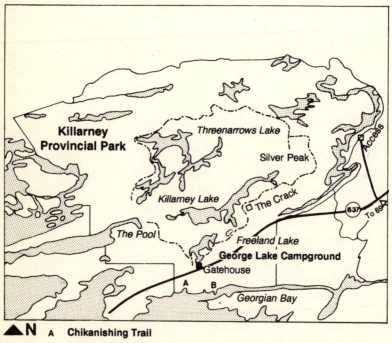

N

- A   Chikanishing Trail
- B   Granite Ridge Trail
- —.—   La Cloche Silhouette Trail

Little wonder. The park is superb hiking and canoeing country, set in a landscape so beautiful that paintings of it are in some of the most valuable art collections. The provincial park here is a 48,500-ha sweep of magnificent wilderness on the north shore of Georgian Bay. It is a rugged land of tiny, crystal-clear lakes and forests, topped by spectacular white quartzite ridges of the LaCloche, or Killarney, Mountains that are visible for many miles.

While Killarney's hiking trails are usually regarded as trails dedicated to the long-distance backpacker, this should not prevent the day-tripper from hiking in this special place. There are four short trails close to the main campground at George Lake. It is also possible to hike the first and last sections of the 100-km LaCloche Silhouette Trail, although you must walk out and back by the same route. Experienced and fit hikers should have no trouble reaching some of the interest points on these stretches. In addition, there are unlimited hiking opportunities on many of the open ridges in the park that are accessible after some short climbs.

Unless you want to, you don't even have to rough it overnight in the campground, but can be pampered at one of the nearby lodges. Because you are hiking in rugged country, you should have good footwear and a pack to hold drinks, insect repellent and sunscreen.

The short trails make good warm-up hikes. One is the **Granite Ridge Trail**, a 90-minute, 2-km loop that involves some uphill climbing. This results in breathtaking views of Georgian Bay to the south and the LaCloche Mountains to the north. The trail starts across the highway from the main campground and crosses the ancient shoreline of glacial Lake Nipissing. An excellent trail guidebook available from the park refers to a nomadic race occupying these beaches while hunting mastodon and caribou. The nearby quartzite rock furnished knives and lance heads. Old pieces of farm machinery and cars around here are relics from a farm that occupied this area from 1858 to the late 1960s. The 1931 Chevrolet was driven here over the ice from Manitoulin Island in 1955.

Where the trail forks, take the path to the right as you start to ascend the ridge. Where it splits again, follow the right-hand trail to the lookouts. To the south is Collins Inlet on Georgian Bay, and the island you can see is Phillip Edward Island. On most days you can see land to the west that is part of Manitoulin Island. To the north is a magnificent view of the park and the LaCloche Range behind the lushly treed valley.

The **Cranberry Bog Trail** is a 4-km loop over mostly flat country, but with a few steep climbs. This trail explores a large bog where there are wildlife viewing opportunities. Some of the scenery encountered on the trail was captured on canvas by members of the Group of Seven and you may recognize some landscapes. The trail passes the tiny lake named for A.Y. Jackson.

The 5-km **Tar Vat Bay Trail** begins beside the gate to the east lighthouse in the village of Killarney. This leads to the spot on the shoreline where commercial fishermen used to tar their nets. You can extend the hike by following the shoreline to the next bay from where there is a marvellous view of the Killarney Ridge. This is also a good vantage point from which to view the renowned sunsets over Manitoulin Island.

Another trail that allows access to Georgian Bay's rugged shoreline is the **Chikanishing Trail**, an approximate 2-km trail that heads along the rocks from Chikanishing Landing. From here you can view the wave-washed rocky outcrops of Georgian Bay.

To get to this trail, drive down the highway 3 km west of the George Lake campground to Chikanishing Road, turn left and continue to the parking lot.

The trail everybody goes to Killarney to hike, of course, is the **LaCloche Silhouette Trail**. This extremely rugged 100-km trail is dedicated to the Group of Seven artist Franklin Carmichael, and is named after his painting, *LaCloche Silhouette*. It takes seven to ten days to complete and loops around the interior of the park, climbing ridges and visiting Silver Peak, the park's highest point.

Experienced day hikers, who are not laden with equipment needed to overnight on the trail, can hike two sections that are accessible from the George Lake Campground. Hikers who can beg, borrow or rent a canoe can make it to Silver Peak and back in one day by canoeing from Bell Lake to an access point and joining the trail from there. From Silver Peak, at 539 m above sea level, there are views of the entire park area, as well as much of Georgian Bay. To the northeast can be seen the city of Sudbury,

45 km away. Rental canoes are available in the village.

The **Baie Fine Section** of the trail is accessed from the west side of the George Lake campground. It is approximately 13 km to the Baie Fine inlet, making a round trip of 26 km. Much will depend, of course, on the fitness of the hiker, the weather, and whether the trip is done during long daylight hours. You can, of course, still enjoy hiking part of this section, even if you don't hike all of it.

Beginning at the Baie Fine Trailhead in the George Lake campground, the trail crosses the Chikanishing Creek and follows an old logging road to Lumsden Lake. It is easy walking here. This continues as far as Acid Lake, although there are some beaver ponds to be crossed. Beaver activity causes fluctuations in water levels on the trail near Acid Lake so be prepared for this.

The route continues north and begins to rise as it ascends the LaCloche Range. At Artist Creek, just past Cave Lake, the creek runs over smooth outcrops of pink granite that have been polished by glaciation. In this area you may meet boaters who have boated along Baie Fine to The Pool. The latter is one of the more popular yachting anchorages on the North Channel. It was also a popular destination of Group of Seven painters A.J. Casson, A.Y. Jackson, Franklin Carmichael and Arthur Lismer, who all painted in this area of the park.

You could turn around here and retrace your steps back to the campground, but if you still have time and energy you may want to continue north a little way. It is very steep but there are stunning views of The Pool from the high vantage points. Retrace your steps to get back to the campground.

Day hikers can also tackle the eastern section of the trail that runs from George Lake to The Crack. The more ambitious and fit actually complete this section, which travels steep slopes.

The trail starts from the east side of the campground at the Silver Peak Trailhead sign. The path starts to climb almost immediately and heads past A.Y. Jackson Lake. From here you can see the white quartzite of Hawk Ridge on the north shore of George Lake. The trail joins the Cranberry Bog loop trail for a short way before continuing through a forest and on to Little Sheguiandah Lake. This is a small gem of a lake surrounded by pink granite walls.

The trail descends to lower land and crosses a beaver dam before reaching Wagon Road Lake. Continuing northeast, the trail passes Freeland Lake. Instead of continuing past, you may wish to walk down to the shore to view the acquatic vegetation. This is a good spot to look for moose and bear.

Climbing steadily the trail reaches a Killarney Lake portage and follows this for a short way before reaching Kakakise Lake and The Crack. This is a striking fissure in the rockface that offers a somewhat daring and perilous ascent to the top of the rugged Killarney Ridge.

Hikers using the LaCloche Silhouette Trail should check in with the park office before setting out. Those overnighting on the trail will need a camping permit and there is a quota system in effect. There is also a can and bottle ban in the interior. More information about the park is available by calling (705) 287-2368.

Cup and Saucer Trail

Manitoulin Island

- **LENGTH:** 7 to 8 km (2 hours)
- **DEGREE OF DIFFICULTY:** Easy to moderate
- **TYPE OF TRAIL:** Loop
- **LOCATION:** West Bay, Manitoulin Island

HOW TO GET THERE:

The trail starts at the junction of Highway 540 and the Bidwell Road, 18 km west of Little Current on the north side of Manitoulin Island. The parking area is on the south side of Highway 540,

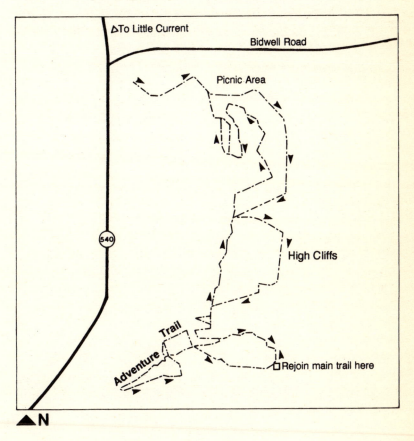

west side of Bidwell Road (gift shop on the east side). Walk west from the parking lot to a sign that shows a trail map.

• • •

Manitoulin Island's Cup and Saucer is not a major hiking trail but it compares favourably with some short sections of the Bruce Trail, and if you are on the island it is just too good to be missed. The views from several lookouts are stunning and for those looking for thrills, the section called the Adventure Trail offers more than you'll need.

This is a superb fall walk because much of Manitoulin is forested with hardwoods and there are views of Killarney's LaCloche Mountains from some of the lookouts. On sunny days it is an artist's palette of colour. From the lookout, the eye takes in the sweep of colourful hardwoods and on the far shore of a dazzling blue North Channel, the LaCloche Mountains gleam white above dark evergreens.

Manitoulin has a number of areas that may interest the hiker. Along with the Cup and Saucer, there's the **M'Chigeeng Trail**, newly developed by the West Bay First Nations on their land at West Bay. This 8-km trail starts at the picnic shelter in the village on the east side of Highway 551. It includes walks through hardwood forests, with a choice of an easy route or a more difficult route to the top of two bluffs where there are scenic lookouts over Mindemoya Lake and the North Channel. The Bear Caves and Fossil Rock Point are two points of interest, and signs along the trail relate aboriginal folklore and legends.

There are other short, developed trails on the island, and many of the sideroads are also quiet enough for enjoyable walking. Kagawong, a small community on the north side of the island, publishes a walking tour brochure of the village. This may be picked up at local stores and outlines local historical attractions, such as early stone houses, a couple of churches and a lighthouse.

The Cup and Saucer Trail is so named because of its unique outline of a small hill (the cup) sitting atop a bigger hill (the saucer). Because of the island terrain, you must drive several kilometres east of the trail on Highway 540 to Honora Bay before being able to view the outline of these limestone cliffs. The cliffs are the northern terminus of the Niagara Escarpment which stretches from Niagara

Cup & Saucer Trail

Falls, running like a spine through southern Ontario and the Bruce Peninsula, and travelling under Georgian Bay to Manitoulin before meeting the massive granite of the Precambrian Shield.

The trail is well marked and the path well worn so it is easy to follow. For those looking for a quick walk, the lower (saucer) section is about 2.7 km, with views from the lower cliffs. From the longer, upper trail, there is a 2-km "adventure hike" that involves climbing up and down sturdy ladders, and inching through rock crevices. If you do this, it wouldn't hurt to have a flashlight along.

At its start, the path rises gently, then levels off as it runs parallel to the road. When it comes to a fork, follow the path on the far right, not the one that makes a sharp right turn. You will notice that the blazes have turned from white to orange now. The walking is superb on a gravelly path through a pleasant, mostly hardwood forest. The call of a blue jay resounds through the trees. At times it is like walking through a bower, the branches forming an arch over the path. The forest floor is colourful with New England aster, purple knapweed, and, depending on the season, Solomon's seal and helleborine. Mushroom lovers will notice an interesting selection of fungi. There are also healthy populations of poison ivy, and you will encounter this plant frequently over the entire trail. In about 1 km a path branches off to the right leading to a picnic area.

The walk has been so easy this far you will wonder whether it is going to live up to its billing of offering high, scenic views. It will. A few metres past the path to the picnic area, the trail runs between scattered huge boulders to the base of a cliff, some 20 m high, which you will realize, with some disbelief, that you are to climb. It turns out to be not as difficult as it looks, due to strategically placed footholds and a rope handrail near the top.

When you reach the top, a trail runs off to the left that you can take to return to the parking lot. The path to the upper trail continues gently uphill. In about 10 minutes you will come to another cliff, about 30 m high, which you will climb to reach the top of the "cup." Again, it is a fairly easy rock climb, veering to the right as it nears the top. A short walk from here brings you to the summit and a sign showing the Adventure Trail leading off to the right, while a lookout trail leads to the left. Take the left fork to the first lookout which is on a broad, flat tableland atop the escarpment, some 60 m above the surrounding country.

The lookout is more than worth the climb. To the north there is the stunning blue of the North Channel, that body of water that sailing enthusiasts compare to the Aegean for its beauty and clarity. Beyond that are the white pine forests of the north shore, capped by the white quartzite ridges of the LaCloche Range. To the south and east Lake Manitou spreads its probing fingers into the forests of this lovely island.

You can walk along the escarpment edge for a little way following the path, but you will need to retrace your steps back to the fork in the path to join the Adventure Trail which explores the west side of the escarpment. If the thought of the Adventure Trail is daunting, you can still enjoy the lookouts on the west side of the escarpment. The return loop of the Adventure Trail follows the top of the escarpment and you can take this, returning by the same way.

The Adventure Trail starts from the side of a lookout overlooking the North Channel. Follow the red arrows which point to a ladder leading down a crevice in the cliff face. You'll find the ladder is quite sturdy, the biggest problem being that first step from the cliff edge to the top step, which requires some body twisting.

From the base of this first section, the trail travels along the sheer face of the escarpment via narrow ledges, up a natural rock chimney, and down into a long, dark and narrow cave-like crevice (where the flashlight will be a godsend) before ascending the cliff once more to pick up the trail atop the escarpment. This is the highest point of the trail, at some 383 m above sea level. Again, the views are stunning, this time over West Bay, with long views to the northwest that you won't soon forget.

On the return trip you must retrace your steps as far as the cliff leading down from the "cup," or higher part of the escarpment. It seems hardly possible that the views on the return trip from the lower (saucer) section of the escarpment are just as outstanding as those from higher up. The return path leads past a series of eight lookouts, and from these you can get good views not only of the surrounding countryside, but of some of the rugged and fascinating rock formations of the upper cliffs that jut out from the cliff face.

From here, it is an easy climb down from the escarpment, using a rope handrail, followed by a short trip back to the parking lot.

The Near North

A.Y. Jackson Lookout Point Trail

• **LENGTH:** 5 km (2 hours) • **DEGREE OF DIFFICULTY:** Moderate
• **TYPE OF TRAIL:** Linear • **LOCATION:** Onaping Falls

HOW TO GET THERE:

Take Highway 144, approximately 30 km north of Sudbury to just south of the town of Onaping Falls. A large sign on the east side of the highway indicates a parking and picnic area.

• • •

This is a short, but very lovely trail if you happen to live in, or be visiting the Sudbury area. Onaping Falls is a tiny mining town north of Sudbury in the transition zone where the southerly

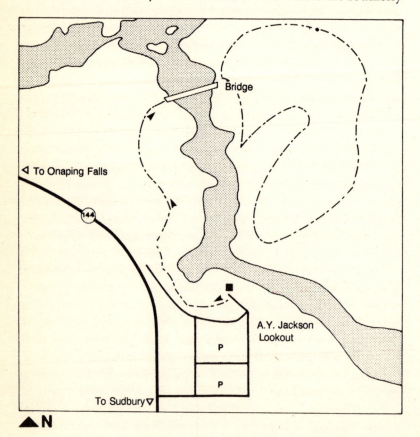

Hiking Ontario's Heartland

Great Lakes–St. Lawrence forest starts to blend into the boreal forest of the north. Located in the heart of the Canadian Shield, it is a beautiful area of high forested ridges and deep, narrow valleys. The Onaping River plunges some 46 m over rugged cliffs, reputedly second only to Niagara Falls in drop.

The A.Y. Jackson Lookout Point Trail was named for the famous member of the Group of Seven painters. The late artist chose the falls as the location for a painting, subsequently donating the painting to the Sudbury Secondary School, from where it was stolen. Ultimately, in a move spearheaded by the school, a plaque was erected on the spot where Jackson is believed to have painted the scene, and the trail dedicated to his memory.

Today, the same views that attracted A.Y. Jackson are popular with camera buffs who want to capture the image on film.

The trail and a parking lot and picnic area with barbecue pits, drinking fountain and washrooms is maintained by the Town of Onaping Falls and the Ontario Ministry of Transportation. The park is one of a number of roadside parks that fall under the jurisdiction of the Transportation ministry.

If you take this trail in summer it is possible to swim near the bottom of the falls, although there is no defined beach. It is a particularly beautiful fall walk, when the brilliant hues of hardwoods blend with the intense, rich evergreens of the pines.

The trail starts north of the parking lot and descends into the deep river valley. The path is well marked and follows a well-travelled path over boulders and packed sand and gravel. There is a lookout at the start of the trail from where there are excellent views of the falls and the river. The falls are particularly impressive after periods of rain, when the river hurls itself over the cataract in clouds of spray, flowing first through canyon-like walls and continuing through high, forested banks.

The trail starts by winding down the slope over rough, rocky steps, which gradually give way to a path that winds through a mixed forest. The path travels generally downhill as it works its way along the high forested banks lining the river, then drops sharply to an observation platform at the head of the falls. Blueberry plants are numerous and heavy with fruit, making the trail a popular destination for berry pickers.

The Near North

The roar of the water frothing and foaming over the rocks grows louder as the trail nears the falls. Trail users like to sit on the boulders close to the water and it is a favourite spot for picnicking.

The steep, rocky path that winds up the side of the falls has handrails at some of the steepest inclines. At the top, there is a footbridge which crosses the river to the forest on the other side, presenting yet more photo opportunities.

The A.Y. Jackson Trail is well marked as far as the falls, but its continuation on the other side is less well marked and maintained because fewer people use it. The trail here forms a loop through the forest. The northern scenery is lovely and it is pleasant to walk through a lonely forest, silent except for the calling of songbirds.

When the trail loops back to the bridge over the falls, you will need to return to the parking lot along the same route you took on your descent to the observation platform. This will probably take you a little longer than the trip down because you will be climbing all the way back.

Seguin Trail

- **LENGTH**: 13 to 61 km (4 hours to several days)
- **DEGREE OF DIFFICULTY**: Easy
- **TYPE OF TRAIL**: Linear • **LOCATION**: Parry Sound

HOW TO GET THERE:

The trail runs roughly east to west between Highways 69 and 11. From the west access is from Highway 69, 6 km south of Oastler Lake Provincial Park (12 km south of Parry Sound). Look for signs on the east side of the highway. From the east, access is from the Fern Glen Road, 6 km west of Highway 11, and 8 km north of Novar. The trail may also be accessed from Highway 518 on the

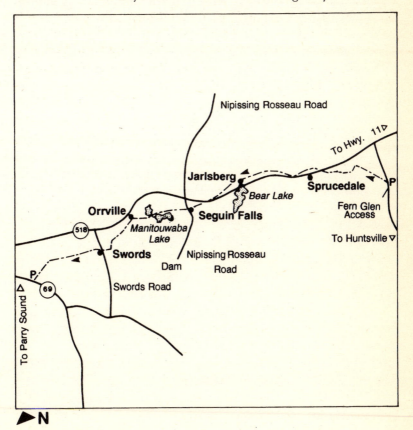

The Near North

stretch that runs between Highway 69 just north of Oastler Lake, and from Highway 11, approximately 2 km north of Emsdale.

• • •

The Seguin Trail follows the bed of the historic Ottawa, Arnprior and Parry Sound Railway across the rugged landscape of the Canadian Shield. Unlike most Shield country trails, however, this is a relatively undemanding route. Workmen took the challenges out of it when they built this railroad through the wilderness more than a century ago. In the days when railroads were being built, surveyors always found the flattest routes, and if rocky ridges got in the way, they simply blasted a hole right through. That's why you'll find yourself walking through rockcuts and close to the shores of small, quiet lakes as you follow this trail into the rugged bush and across the spruce bogs of Georgian Bay and Muskoka cottage country.

It is quiet now, along this track, but once this rail line was a link in a major east-west transportation route. It helped to make fortunes for men like J.R. Booth, its builder, and provided a lifeline for lonely settlers scratching a living from this wilderness.

The coming of the railroad meant that logs from the forest could be moved all year instead of just in spring run-off. Primitive roads that were hacked out of the bush to bring supplies by horse and wagon to lonely settlements were often not passable. Winter's snows and summer's quagmires, as well as the terrain's impossibly high rocky ridges, were constant obstacles. The railroad changed all that. The O.A.P & S line, usually referred to as the Booth Railroad, was built by lumber baron J.R. Booth. It linked U.S. ports and western grain centres with markets in the east through a port at Depot Harbour on Georgian Bay, eventually becoming the Canada Atlantic Railway and one of Canada's busiest lines.

J.R. Booth located his railroad in this particular location in a fit of shrewd one-upmanship. In the planning stages, it was destined to have its terminus in the town of Parry Sound, but speculators drove up the price of land so much he moved it south to Parry Island. This move disappointed the townsfolk of Parry Sound who had hoped for this convenient link. The line was closed in 1955 and the tracks, bridges and culverts removed by the end of that year. In 1969, in a remarkable display of foresight, the Ontario Department of Lands & Forests (now the Ministry of Natural Resources) acquired the right of way to the corridor. They replaced fourteen bridges and created the Seguin Trail for use by snowmobilers. Today it is a popular summer trail for hikers, cyclists and equestrians. A very few, short sections are open to vehicles where it is used to access summer cottages.

Signs of its past history still appear along the route as ghost towns and tiny cottage communities. One is Seguin Falls, which once prospered, serving the lumber industry and American tourists seeking wilderness adventure. Now, little but the foundation of the 1897 King George hotel remains, its structure having been lost to a fire several years ago. Bearing in mind that it is private property, hikers can poke around the foundations but should watch out for bits of broken glass and nails. The church and school have gone but a few old homes now used as summer cottages are a mute reminder of the busy days of past industry and settlement. Other tiny communities on the route are Orrville, Bear Lake and Sprucedale but there are no services. This means there are no places to buy lunch or a cold drink, or gasoline if you are driving Highway 518 to access the route.

The proximity of Highway 518 provides ample opportunity to hike short sections of the Seguin Trail, since the old rail bed crosses and re-crosses the highway frequently. The best sections will need some car jockeying. The most popular is the 13-km section between Orrville and Seguin Falls. This skirts a number of small, pretty lakes including Manitouwaba Lake, where there are primitive Crown land campsites. This is the trail's most popular campsite and can be busy on weekends. On quiet weekdays, though, you can watch colonies of loons fishing, and sometimes slip into the lake for a skinny dip. The best arrangement would be to leave a vehicle just south of Highway 518 at the junction of the Seguin Trail and the Nipissing Road, and have someone drop you at Orrville so that you can walk the trail back.

An alternative is the 13-km section between Highway 69 and the Swords Road, which again will need car jockeying. This section is more isolated than the Seguin Falls section. The Seguin Trail travels through typical Canadian Shield country of rocky outcroppings, beaver dams and marshes, and lakes where you can fish for pike. It passes through mixed forests of pine, maple, birch and aspen where there are lots of opportunities for wildlife viewing. You'll travel past lakes bordered by Labrador tea and in old, deserted settlement areas, see lilacs and orange lilies that were planted by pioneer women to remind them of a home far across the ocean.

An attraction of the Seguin Trail is that a number of tracks or logging roads run off it at various points, which makes it an ideal spot to set up camp for a few days of exploration.

One of these is the Nipissing Colonization Road, now known as the Nipissing–Rosseau Road. This intersects the Seguin Trail at Seguin Falls and offers hiking opportunities in one or two sections. Surveyed in 1865, it brought settlers to free land grants in this area and all the way to its terminus at Nipissing. Sections of it exist as gravel township roads, other sections as narrow tracks where the original corduroy roadbed can still be seen.

A section travels south from Seguin Falls on a little-used gravel road for several kilometres passing isolated lakes that are great for swimming. It crosses a river then turns into a sandy track bordered by young pines, which give off their sharp, northern forest scent. You can follow this path until it is interrupted by a dam where there is a private wildlife sanctuary that is frequented by great blue herons.

The best spot to set up a camp from which to explore other areas of the Seguin Trail is on Lake Manitouwaba, which may be driven to. Travel east on Highway 518 about 17 km past Orrville, to the South Seguin Estates Road. Turn right, then look on the right for the sign marking the entrance to the Seguin Trail. Drive along this section of trail until you come to a lake on both sides of the trail. There are campsites on both sides.

Southwestern

REGIONAL OVERVIEW

Ontario's "Deep South" lies roughly between Lakes Huron and Erie. This is prime crop- and fruit-growing land, known as the Garden of Ontario. Most of the lands are privately owned so the hiking trails that do exist are a precious resource. This is the place to hike in the Carolinian Forest, which is the forest zone that extends northwards from the Carolinas to bring to Southwestern Ontario such species as tulip trees and sassafras.

Three of the major volunteer hiking trails in the province exist in the area. The **Thames Valley Trail** is a 56-km trail that runs southwest through the valley of the Thames River between St. Marys and Wardsville. It passes through **Fanshawe Conservation Area**, then through Springbank Park and the University of Western Ontario campus in the city of London. It travels through farmland and along steep river banks through mostly private lands. The Thames Valley Trail Association has recently been successful in establishing trails in the new Komoka Provincial Park, west of London. More details are available from the association by writing to the address listed in the Appendix.

The Thames Valley Trail connects with the **Avon Trail** at St. Marys, making it another link in the vast network of Ontario volunteer trails that interconnect. An excellent guidebook is available.

A little further north is the **Maitland Trail** which follows the lovely Maitland River from Auburn to Goderich on Lake Huron. The trail association can provide a detailed map which also shows nearby hiking areas, such as the **Hullett Wildlife Refuge** near Clinton. Others are the **Saratoga Swamp**, **Point Farms Provincial Park**, and **The Huron County Forest**, all just a little north of Goderich.

The **Elgin Trail** which runs between Port Stanley and St. Thomas is detailed in the following pages.

The **Lynn Valley Trail**, a 10-km linear trail between the town of Simcoe and Port Dover is new. It travels through Carolinian forest along an abandoned railway. It is still in its infancy and needs volunteers. For more information call Hike Ontario! at the number listed in the Appendix.

Not far west of the Lynn Valley Trail is the **Townsend Trail**. This is a 13.6-km loop trail between the hamlet of Rockford in the north and Townsend in the south. Owned on land assembled by the Ontario Land Corporation for the new community of Townsend, it follows the valley of the winding Nanticoke Creek. You can access the trail at its southern end from the CNR railway bridge in the village centre, west of the junctions of Highways 3 and 6. The northerly access point is between the 11th and 12th Concessions, south of Rockford. More information is available from the City of Nanticoke Recreation Department at (519) 583-0890.

Rock Point Provincial Park near Port Maitland on Lake Erie offers walking trails in the Carolinian forest and along the beach. The trails also connect with the Grand Valley Trail at its southern terminus. A similar experience can be had farther west at **Wheatley Provincial Park**, where you can walk through thick hardwood forests and through marshy areas around a creek system. On Lake Huron, **Pinery Provincial Park** offers nine trails, incorporating beach, forest and a unique Oak Savannah Prairie ecosystem. White-tailed deer are plentiful and unafraid. More information about these parks can be obtained from the Ministry of Natural Resources address listed in the Appendix.

A conservation area worth checking out is **Springwater**, operated by the Kettle Creek Conservation Authority. This offers more than 8 km of trails through mature Carolinian Forest in the Springwater Forest and neighbouring Jaffa Tract.

Avon Trail

Harmony to Wildwood Reservoir, Stratford

- **LENGTH:** 18 km (5 to 6 hours)
- **DEGREE OF DIFFICULTY:** Moderate
- **TYPE OF TRAIL:** Linear • **LOCATION:** Stratford

HOW TO GET THERE:

Take Perth County Road 23, southeast of Stratford. The trail starts from a farm gate on the south side of the road, 250 m west of Harmony. Park on the shoulder. The trail ends south of Wildwood Reservoir, off County Road 28, one concession west of Oxford Road. Go north towards the lake and park near a yellow gate.

• • •

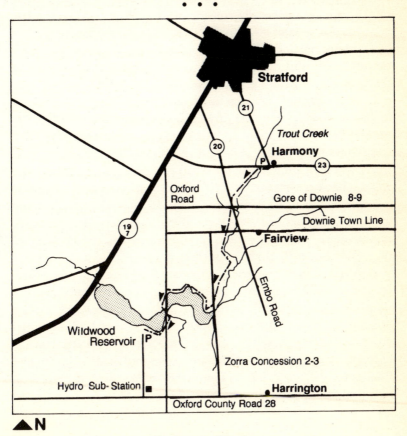

Southwestern Ontario

The Avon Trail is a 100-km trail that connects with the Thames Valley Trail at its western end, and with the Grand Valley Trail at its eastern end. It is another link in the vast network of trails that hikers have forged across southern Ontario. It runs between Conestogo and St. Marys and, thanks to the generosity of private landowners, traverses private lands all the way except for a 13-km section through Wildwood Conservation Area.

This section of the Avon travels the lovely, lush countryside of rural southwestern Ontario, where rich soils and an amiable climate combine for a veritable garden. The trail leads across farm fields and through woods where rampant growth threatens to take over everything. It is rated "moderate" mainly due to the distance involved, because it is fairly easy walking. There are a couple of stream crossings where you might get wet feet, and it is surprisingly hilly for an area generally considered to be flat. If you don't live near the Avon Trail you may wish to consider booking into one of the many bed and breakfast accommodations Stratford is famous for, walk the trail during the day, and at night take in a Royal Shakespearean theatre production. The walk will have earned you a decadent dinner. What a weekend!

The trail starts near the tiny village of Harmony, southeast of Stratford on County Road 21. It generally follows the winding Trout Creek and ends in the Wildwood Conservation Area. The trail is marked by a white blaze until you enter the conservation area, when it becomes orange. Avon Trail members have done a sterling job blazing and maintaining the trail. Because of the rapid plant growth, many sections would be difficult to negotiate without this maintenance. You may wish to enquire about trail conditions from the trail association before tackling it.

As it is a linear trail you will need to do some juggling with cars. Shorter sections can be hiked because the trail crosses a number of sideroads. Most of these sideroads are quiet enough to allow parking on the shoulder. In fact, the entire trail is so quiet you are unlikely to see anyone on it, apart from a few cows.

Start the walk from a farm gate in the middle of an avenue of maples on the south side of County Road 23, west of Harmony. The trail cuts down the centre of the field and passes an abandoned farmhouse before heading downhill and turning right to start on

Hiking Ontario's Heartland

its way westwards. This is pleasant, gently rolling country with woodlots here and there. Trail markers are painted on everything from rocks and trees to hydro poles to ensure the hiker does not get lost.

After turning west you will catch your first glimpse of Trout Creek to your left. It is a small watercourse at this point, close to its source which is northeast of Harmony. You will encounter the creek on numerous occasions on the first half of your walk. It absorbs smaller watercourses and becomes a creek of some significance before it loses itself in the waters of Wildwood Reservoir.

The trail follows the creek a short way before making a sharp right turn up a steep bank, then turns west again and travels along the top of the bank until it reaches a post with a double blaze. Turn left and head into the bush until the trail crosses first a stile and then a bridge over the creek.

Following the curve of the creek, the trail winds through meadows at the rear of a couple of rural homes and ends at the Gore of Downie Concession 8-9. You have now walked approximately 3 km.

Cross the bridge and walk the few metres to the junction of Embro Road and turn left. Cross Embro Road and walk past the Camp Bimini property until you see the double blaze that indicates a right turn. The path leads into the bush and along the high banks of a creek to the edge of a meadow where blue flags grow in the marshy ground.

Soon the trail crosses an old wooden bridge and enters a forest where ostrich ferns grow and lush growth covers low ridges. The path meanders away from the creek and back again before emerging onto a ploughed field. The trail edges around two more fields where numerous large deer tracks indicate regular visits by these shy animals.

Leaving the fields the trail makes a sharp left turn and presents its first challenge. This is a stream with no bridge. The best way to negotiate it is to climb up the bank on the right and find the stepping stones. These are a bit slippery but not life threatening.

The trail continues over another small stream and along the edge of a bush until it emerges at the Downie Town Line. Turn right, cross the road and walk about 500 m before looking for a blaze on a hydro pole showing a turn to the left.

You will now enter a very pretty stretch of the trail where there are old apple trees and shrubs, and plants like may-apple. After crossing a small stream the trail encounters Trout Creek again and climbs up and then down a fairly high, long ridge. The trail skirts another ploughed field which is also obviously popular with deer, before entering the woods again.

When you emerge you will find yourself at the edge of a quarry. Turn left onto a dirt road that leads past the quarry and look for the double blaze on the right where there is a stile. Cross the stile and follow the fence line downhill and across a worked-out quarry. Soon the trail intersects with excellent paths maintained by the Tavistock Rod and Gun Club.

These trails lead to the clubhouse and if there is no-one around you can lunch here using their picnic table. There is also a privy behind the clubhouse. If members are around, do ask permission before using their facilities. You will now have hiked about 9 km, which is roughly half-way.

The trail continues up the driveway at the back of the clubhouse until it emerges onto Zorra Township Concession 2-3, a paved sideroad. Turn left and walk down the road until you come to a bridge. At the bridge, look for a sign on your right indicating that the trail is leaving the road. The path climbs uphill and turns to the right along the top edge of a pine forest. Nice views of rolling countryside to the rear. Here the smell of pines mingles with the scent of peppermint. The trail continues along the edge of a woodlot and then enters a cornfield.

At the end of this field the path swings to the right and follows an easily walked farm path for a couple of kilometres before reaching a yellow gate at a sideroad. Turn right and follow the sideroad up an extremely long hill. At the top, at the end of the fence line, turn into the bush again on your left. The path runs between a field and a pine forest. About 100 m short of the end of the field, look for orange streamers to the left and turn into the woods.

Emerging from the woods the path comes to the Gore of Downie Oxford Road and turns left to walk over the causeway that spans the Wildwood Reservoir. This is a favourite haunt of anglers and great blue herons. At the bottom of the hill, turn westwards into the conservation area lands, following the orange blaze. You are now roughly one hour from the end of the trail.

You will walk for about 2 km through a very marshy area, with lots of rough boardwalk and planking underfoot. This is a good area to watch for blue flag and small snakes. The lake can be glimpsed through the trees. The rest of the walk continues through pine plantations and areas of mixed hardwoods until it ends at the gravel road just north of where you left your car.

Elgin Trail

- **LENGTH**: 6 to 35 km (2 hours to 3 days)
- **DEGREE OF DIFFICULTY**: Moderate to challenging
- **TYPE OF TRAIL**: Linear • **LOCATION**: St. Thomas–Port Stanley

HOW TO GET THERE:

To access the trail near St. Thomas, take Highway 401 to Highway 4. Drive south on Highway 4 to the junction of Highway 3 at Talbotville. Drive west on Highway 3, 3 km to Payne's Mills. Park in front of Payne's Mills Barn, on the south side of the highway. To access the trail from Port Stanley, follow Highway 4 south to where it ends in the village of Port Stanley on Lake Erie. Drive into the village and over the main bridge, then turn west

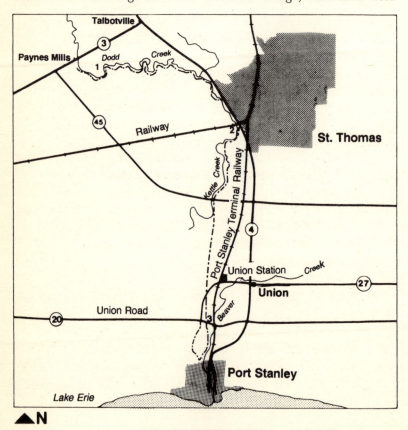

Hiking Ontario's Heartland

and pass the Port Stanley Terminal Railway Station, turn right at Carlow Road and drive about 750 m past the Port Stanley Public School. Enter the trail on the west side of Carlow Road. Parking is permitted in the school parking lot on weekends only.

• • •

The Elgin Trail rambles through southern Ontario Carolinian forests and farmlands, generally following Kettle Creek as it absorbs its feeder streams and finally empties into Lake Erie at Port Stanley. The trail passes through an ecosystem unique to this part of Canada due to its geographic location and a microclimate influenced by its proximity to this most southerly of the Great Lakes. The Elgin, in turn, is the most southerly of the major hiking trails that were built and continue to be maintained by volunteer groups. Like the others, it travels mainly on private lands so it is essential that hikers stay on marked trails to avoid conflict with landowners. Except for a few short sections, the trail is unexpectedly rugged and boots are advisable.

The trail's proximity to a network of highways and secondary roads makes it easy to access a number of sections, and loops can be fashioned using some of these quiet sideroads. To take full advantage of the trail's rural atmosphere, though, you should be prepared to do some car jockeying.

There is one exception. The Port Stanley Terminal Railway that once was part of the London & Port Stanley Railroad now offers a 45-minute scenic train ride north from Port Stanley to Union Station, at which point it intersects with the trail. Provided you knew the train schedule, you could take a 2-hour hike on the Elgin Trail north from Port Stanley and ride the train back.

For the purposes of a day's outing, the Elgin could be divided roughly into three sections.

The first is a popular 3-to-4 hour 12-km linear hike from the trail's northern terminus at Payne's Mills, ending at the western end of the busy little town of St. Thomas. You should leave one car at Payne's Mills and the other at the intersection of Highway 4 and the Fingal Road (County Road 16) underneath the railway bridge. This was the last section of the trail to be added, being completed in the late 1980s.

From Payne's Mills, the trail heads southward, following white blazes through a beautiful avenue of fir trees. Near the railroad tracks it starts to veer east until it connects with Dodd Creek, which it follows in a meandering fashion to Lyle Sideroad. This is one section where it is possible to do a loop hike by turning left and following Lyle Sideroad back to Highway 3, for an easy 90-minute total walk on good paths.

At Lyle Sideroad, Dodd Creek veers northwestward while the trail traverses down the side of a field near a thicket until it meets the creek again. For about the next 5 km, the trail roughly parallels Dodd Creek as it bends and twists its way towards its confluence with Kettle Creek. Beaver dams are common and if you do this walk in April or May there is a magnificent variety of spring wildflowers. An hour or so after leaving Lyle Sideroad the trail passes through property belonging to a horse farm. It is essential that you close the gate behind you and walk along the fence line, following the white blazes. There are usually about six horses grazing in the field, but don't be alarmed if they approach. They are not afraid of hikers and are curious creatures, often sniffing for apples in a hiker's pocket or pack.

From the horse farm to St. Thomas the hills increase in height and difficulty. Walking can be challenging here and if it has been wet it can be extremely slippery. The trail passes through gorgeous Carolinian forests that are full of white-tailed deer.

When you hear the muted sounds of traffic in the distance you are near the end of this section of the Elgin trail which descends under the old trestle bridge and emerges onto the Fingal Road, west of Kettle Creek.

If you are interested, a 2-block walk up the hill to the east takes you to the Jumbo monument. This is a life-sized statue of the famous circus elephant which was killed here by a train in 1885.

From the newest part of the Elgin Trail, we go for a second hike to a section in the middle, south of St. Thomas, which was the original trail. This section, started in 1974, was the first to be blazed, and formed the entire Elgin Trail for several years. This popular 2-hour 6-km stretch runs north from Highway 45 to St. Thomas. It follows the east bank of Kettle Creek for most of the way and while the path is well-packed earth there are a few creeks where there are no bridges, so be prepared to negotiate these. It may be walked all year, but is particularly beautiful in the fall.

Park one car at the St. Thomas entrance to the trail, which is on Highway 4, just north of a cemetery and close to a car wash which is partially obscured by a strip mall. Park the second on the shoulder of County Road 45, 1 km west of Highway 4.

Walking from south to north, access the trail from the north side of County Road 45 on the east bank of Kettle Creek, where there is an Elgin Trail sign. About 10 minutes in, down beside the stream, look for some Osage orange trees. These hedge-sized trees are members of the mulberry family named after their native Osage region of Arkansas. The trees bear thorns and small orange-shaped fruit which is inedible.

The trail continues along Kettle Creek and after edging along an open cornfield there is a spectacular view of the Kettle Creek floodplain to the west. Canada geese are a common sight in the spring and fall along this part of the trail, and white-tailed deer are frequently seen. From here, the trail travels through several interesting stands of trees, starting with a spectacular grove of beeches with leaves that are a brilliant burnt sienna colour in fall.

The trail travels down a hill from the beech grove and climbs up another hill into a red pine plantation, passes through it and then travels along the edge of a white pine plantation as it descends to a cornfield and goat farm. You are now roughly half-way along the trail. On climbing the next steep hill, look for witch hazel trees or shrubs, which are unique in Ontario because they bear both flowers and fruit in November. The next interesting section is through some sand dunes where, in the fall, there is a spectacular collection of fall colours in the mature Carolinian forest that surrounds the dunes. At times, when the trail travels in low sections close to the creek, you can see buffalo from a nearby game farm grazing on the other side.

Continuing through a mature Carolinian forest the trail comes to a fork where you should keep to the right. This will lead you back to the car parked at the car wash. If you should miss this turn, the trail would lead you 1 km farther north to Highway 4 and from here it is a short walk back down the highway to the car wash.

Southwestern Ontario

The final section of the trail offers opportunities for a 2-hour loop hike starting from the Port Stanley Public School on Carlow Road and walking north on Carlow to a junction with the trail, then returning on the trail.

Leaving your car at the school, follow Carlow Road until it becomes County Road 20 (Union Road). Along the way you will have views of a marina, trees and orchards. Two km north of the school, the road turns west to go up a hill. There is an Elgin Trail sign on your left where you should turn onto the trail, which from here winds over hilly terrain 5 km back to Port Stanley.

This section travels through mature Carolinian forest with an abundance of maple, beech, elm, black cherry, walnut and ash trees. In spring, the trilliums here are possibly the largest in Ontario, having grown to that size because of the temperate climate.

At the start of the second hill watch for a clump of sassafras trees, that Carolinian specie that bears a crop of varied-shaped leaves. Although the trail is mostly hilly there is one marsh to be negotiated and boots are recommended.

After crossing a gravel road the trail goes through a fish hatchery operated by a local fish and game club and members are happy to give you a tour, if they are around.

Just before the trail ends there is a spectacular view overlooking Kettle Creek and the village of Port Stanley. Port Stanley itself is a quaint little fishing community with two fine public beaches, interesting boutiques, and restaurants.

Point Pelee National Park

- **LENGTH:** 1 to 16 km (1 to 5+ hours)
- **DEGREE OF DIFFICULTY:** Easy
- **TYPE OF TRAIL:** Loop • **LOCATION:** Leamington

HOW TO GET THERE:

Take Highway 401 to Highway 77 west of Tilbury. Go south on Highway 77 to Wheatley. Follow signs to Regional Road 33 and to the park.

• • •

Nature lovers will want to hike the trails at least once in this national park at the southernmost tip of Canada's mainland. For hikers who are also birders, once may not be enough.

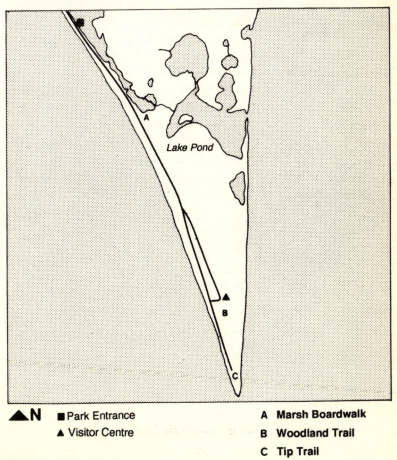

Lake Pond

▲N ■ Park Entrance   A Marsh Boardwalk
     ▲ Visitor Centre   B Woodland Trail
                                            C Tip Trail

Point Pelee, a spit of land that plunges southwards into Lake Erie, is renowned for bird viewing, particularly during spring and fall migrations. During September, it is also the place to see monarch butterflies by the hundreds as they gather and pause before their long flight to South America.

Point Pelee is also a magnet for plant lovers. The Carolinian forest that reaches its northern range in this part of southern Ontario is at its most prominent in Point Pelee. Trees such as sassafras with its varied-shaped leaves, tulip tree, which looks gorgeous in spring, and sycamore are abundant. This little corner of Ontario's ''Deep South'' also nourishes a fine crop of prickly pear cactus. Not really that surprising for an area of Ontario that shares the same latitude as Northern California, Rome and Barcelona.

W.H. Ballou, in 1877, discoverer of bird migration patterns, found that Point Pelee was on the Mississippi flyway. Mr. Ballou realized that the ruby-throated hummingbird, as well as numerous warblers, and hawks would stop here before tackling the flight across Lake Erie.

Walking is actually the best way to see this small park, although good roads encourage driving and there is also a free bus. There are numerous short-looped interpretive trails in the park, the longest being the 2.75-km Woodland Nature Trail. An 8-km trail goes from the Marsh Boardwalk to the visitor centre on a path that runs parallel to the park road, making a 16-km return trip. The trail is also used by cyclists. You can add a further 3 km by walking down to the tip of the peninsula, rather than riding the free park bus.

The Woodland Nature Trail, which starts from the back door of the visitor centre, is a good interpretive trail to introduce hikers to the Carolinian forest. A published guide booklet is available to borrow or buy.

A wide path, for walkers only, leads between a riot of plants. Thick vines, some heavy with grapes, wrap themselves around tall trees and bushes, often becoming trees themselves. Morning glories send creepers shooting upwards, their trumpet-shaped flowers reaching for the sun. Other vines are Virginia creeper and even poison ivy which manifests itself as a vine here. The mosquito breeds intensely. Other wildlife species that live in the park include the large, red fox snake and the opossum.

Wildflowers growing on the edge of this lush forest are lovely. Pink bouncing Bet, tall blue bellflower and lopseed make a bright border to the dark green foliage.

Here and there, swamps give the impression that an alligator may soon make an appearance, so "Deep South" is the atmosphere. Instead, a small blue flash zips across a boardwalk. It is the five-lined skink, Ontario's only lizard, and usually very shy.

Warblers flit about the trees, but, the foliage is so luxurious, they vanish before it is possible to identify them. A slim, glossy black snake slithers across the path. This is the melanistic eastern garter snake. About 25 per cent of the garter snakes in the park have a pigmentation condition that causes them to be black.

Along with the more commonly recognized Carolinian forest species is the spicebush. In autumn, this tree is easily identified by gorgeous flame-red berries that light up the greenery of the forest.

At one section of the trail the reed-like horsetail fern is widespread and you will notice a number of passageways going through it where the plant has been flattened. These trails are made by the park's herd of white-tailed deer. Lack of natural predators and abundant food encourage rapid growth of deer populations in this area. So far, Point Pelee National Park staff have managed to keep the herd to a manageable size. If allowed to, the deer herd would grow so large it would literally eat itself out of house and home, starving itself and endangering the Carolinian forest.

Point Pelee's staging area for migrating birds and butterflies is the southernmost tip of the peninsula. To get there you can walk south from the visitor centre along the park road. There is no traffic except for the park bus. The landscape en route is similar to that on the upper portion of the peninsula until you reach the bus terminus. Here there is a small interpretive centre and washrooms. You can walk to the very tip of the peninsula by following the Tip Trail. This is a loop trail that goes down to the point, travelling by boardwalk one way and returning via the beach, although the sand makes for hard walking and it is often very windy. The boardwalk is sheltered by bush and it is here that you will see the migrating flocks.

The interpretive centre display is changed according to migration patterns. In September, the sharp-shinned hawk and monarch butterflies top the park's lineup. Even the casual visitor cannot fail to notice the hawks as a number of the raptors ride the thermal air currents overhead. Meanwhile, on the boardwalk, a cyclist rides by, scattering dozens of butterflies.

Park signs caution visitors not to swim because of the dangerous currents. It is hardly surprising. The waves beat unceasingly on the shore, rolling in towards the slim "V" of sand that marks the southernmost tip of the mainland.

The Marsh Boardwalk on the upper peninsula is another must for any hiker. This is located 2 km from the park entrance, and is a 1.4-km walk into the extensive Lake Erie marshes. The boardwalk travels through high cattails, with glimpses of marsh life close to the boardwalk. A small turtle suns itself on a large lilypad. Here and there, you can see where raccoons have trampled through the cattails, carving passages on the thick carpet of roots. At the southernmost point, there is a viewing tower, which offers an extensive view of the marshes, as far as the eye can see. At the end of the trail on the return trip, climb the high wooden viewing tower and take a look through a powerful telescope for more views of this incredibly large marsh that is such an integral part of this great lake.

South Point Trail

Rondeau Provincial Park

- **LENGTH:** 8 km (2 hours) • **DEGREE OF DIFFICULTY:** Easy
  • **TYPE OF TRAIL:** Loop • **LOCATION:** Blenheim

HOW TO GET THERE:

Take Highway 401 to Highway 15 southeast of Chatham. Turn south on Highway 15 and follow it to Eatonville where Highway 15 becomes Highway 51. Continue south to Rondeau Provincial Park. Drive through the park 8 km to the start of the trail.

• • •

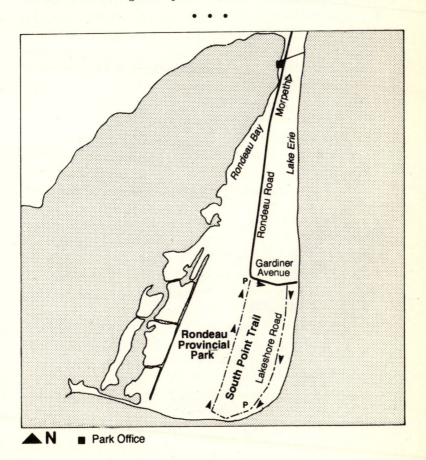

▲ N   ■ Park Office

Hiking in Rondeau Provincial Park is not like hiking anywhere else in southern Ontario. For openers there aren't too many trails that trace the edge of an inland sea, where the crashing of waves on the beach drowns out the birdsong, and where the hiker can expect to see a couple of dozen deer and other species of wildlife. There is also a remarkable collection of birdlife—of all the species seen in Ontario, 80 per cent have been recorded in Rondeau. The park is the site of Canada's largest breeding ground of the rare prothonotary warbler.

Then there's the plantlife. Although the large herd of deer is doing its best to eat most of it, the Carolinian forest here is home to tulip trees that bear lovely spring blossoms, sassafras, and some 19 species of orchids, including the prized nodding pogonia.

Known as "Pointe Aux Pins" by early explorers, the 3,254-ha park now occupying the whole of the point was named "Ronde Eau" (round water) by French missionaries who camped under the pines. The round water refers to the inner harbour. Rondeau is the second oldest in the provincial park system, dating back to 1894. In the early days, people were encouraged to build cottages on leased land along the waterfront and today, some 300 cottages remain.

Because Rondeau occupies a sandspit which curves southwestwards into Lake Erie it is favoured by having shoreline on three sides. There are five trails in the park and each is designed to introduce the hiker to the different faces of Rondeau. The Spicebush Trail, for example, is a short one that acquaints the hiker with the ecology of a southern hardwood forest. A linear trail (15 km return) leads the hiker through the middle of extensive marshes on the Rondeau bay side of the spit.

Hiking Ontario's Heartland

The South Point Trail explores the southernmost reaches of the park and offers a variety of experiences, not to mention a walk along a lovely, deserted beach. On a day when Rondeau's popular beaches are crowded, there will be few, if any, people on the southern beaches. You can swim here, but treat Lake Erie with respect since undertows have been known to endanger swimmers.

The South Point Trail is reached after an 8-km drive from the park gate. As you enter the park you will see the inner harbour on your right. Follow the park road (Rondeau Road) to its junction with Gardiner Avenue, then turn right at the visitor centre onto Lakeshore Road and drive past the summer cottages to a parking lot at the beginning of the trail. There is a privy in the parking lot.

The trail starts from the northwest corner of the parking lot, where there is a large sign, and follows a wide path that once was an asphalt road. The tree canopy is open at first, allowing tall grasses to flourish, from where cicadas chirp incessantly. Here and there the odd tall pine bears witness to the vast pine forests that drew the first white explorers. Most of the trees are Carolinean species: sassafras, dogwood and elderberry. A catbird utters its peculiar cry. Soon the buzz of the cicadas is drowned out by the persistent pounding of waves on the beach and the lake comes into view on the left. A strip of swampy land separates the path from the beach, but after about 100 m or so it is possible to follow a small side path down towards the lake.

The beach is a long sandy strip, about 50 m wide, strewn here and there with huge tree trunks and roots that form fanciful patterns, giving the beach a wild, deserted look. The pounding surf beats a constant tattoo against the shore, almost drowning out the cries of a common tern as it wheels low above the waves.

The beach appears to stretch to infinity, but to continue the trail you should probably only walk for about 100 m before cutting over the narrow grassy strip to get back onto the path.

The trail continues alongside the lake and crosses a boardwalk over marshes and sand dunes. In about 500 m the path turns eastwards away from the lake and skirts a slough where cattails and Joe pye-weed grow. There is also a healthy crop of mosquitos, even in early fall.

The sloughs of Rondeau are notable because they provide habitat for much of its wildlife. The area here, for example, is a nesting spot for the prothonotary warbler, which nests in abandoned woodpecker holes in dead trees. The colourful wood duck, which also likes to nest in dead trees, is commonly seen here. A small black snake slithers across the path and frogs sing from the middle of the slough.

After swinging around the edge of the slough and along its edge for some 200 m, the path enters the Carolinian forest and we recognize the familiar leaves of the tulip tree, and sassafras. Here and there enormous old oaks tower into the sky. Many of the trees look as if they are in danger of being strangled by grape vines that literally drip with fruit. An enormous number of huge, dead trees litter the forest floor. Soon it is noticeable that the undergrowth and lower branches of the trees have been eaten by the ever-growing herd of Rondeau white-tailed deer. Except for a few ferns, which obviously are not a favourite food, the undergrowth is non-existent, giving the forest a peculiarly bare look.

As if to prove their existence, two deer that had been peering at us from behind some branches scamper off, their white flags up. A little further on, we see an eight-point stag with his harem of five does grazing on the sparse grass to our right. Three flickers flash in front of us, a blue jay announces our arrival and two prothonotary warblers zip among the branches. Despite the arid appearance of the forest, this is an incredibly rich ecosystem. We start to count the deer and reach 21 before the path meets the junction of Rondeau Road and Gardiner Avenue at the half-way point of the trail.

The trail passes through a small picnic area and parking lot, then turns left onto Gardiner Avenue, which runs south about 2 km to the visitor centre. Gardiner is used by cottagers and beachgoers but the road is fairly quiet. The friendly call of an Eastern wood peewee can be heard from the woods, and deer numbers 22, 23 and 24 bound across the road closely followed by four raccoons.

At the visitor centre parking lot there is a path which turns left and leads back through the woods to the head of the trail. You can follow this, or, if the mosquitos are bad, you can turn left past the visitor centre and follow Lakeshore Road back to your car.

Just to the east of the visitor centre, a public beach is sheltered from the road by rolling dunes, offering another opportunity for a swim.

Returning via Lakeshore Road on the last 2-km leg of the hike you are presented with yet another of Rondeau's many faces—its cottage life. These traditional summer cottages, many with wide, screened porches, hug the shoreline. Between the cottage gardens you can see Lake Erie's breakers crashing onto the long, sand beach. The cottage lawns, flowers, and shrubs attract the hungry white-tailed deer and they may be seen at dusk, munching on plants and sometimes reclining like ornaments on many a cottage lawn.

Tiger Dunlop Trail

• **LENGTH:** 9 to 10 km (3+ hours) • **DEGREE OF DIFFICULTY:** Easy
• **TYPE OF TRAIL:** Linear • **LOCATION:** Goderich

HOW TO GET THERE:

Follow Highway 21 until it becomes Victoria Street in downtown Goderich. Turn west onto West Street and drive towards the harbour. Turn left at the Harbour Beach Recreation Area and drive towards the old Goderich railroad station. The trail starts at the railroad station, which now belongs to the Maitland Trail Association.

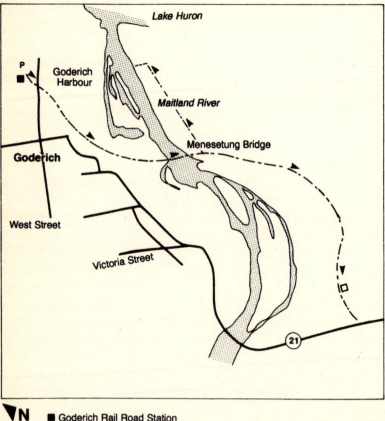

▼N ■ Goderich Rail Road Station
  □ Tiger Dunlop Tomb

The Tiger Dunlop Trail was developed only through the dogged persistence and ingenuity of a group of Goderich residents who refused to let a local historical landmark die. Dr. William "Tiger" Dunlop, founder of Goderich, and known as a man of action and indomitable spirit, would have approved.

The historic Menesetung bridge over the Maitland River that once was the longest rail bridge in Ontario was scheduled to be demolished by its owners, Canadian Pacific Railway, after the company abandoned the Goderich to Guelph rail line in 1987. Demolition was scheduled to be completed by early 1990. A handful of Goderich residents, many of whom were members of the Maitland Trail Association, saw the potential of converting the old railroad corridor into a trail. The problem was, if the bridge went, an attractive portion of the trail would be lost and access to the rest of it would be difficult.

A hastily formed Menesetung Bridge Association, joined by the local Kinsmen Club, a Goderich branch of the Royal Canadian Legion, corporations, and individual citizens, went into action. The goal was to raise the money to save the bridge and construct a walkway along it. One of the first steps was to secure access rights to both the bridge and the abandoned rail beds on either side of it. The group paid $18,000 for the salvage rights to the bridge. The total cost was $120,000, but only because the design and planning and much of the construction labour were donated. Supporters raised much of the money by "buying" railing sections for $120 and planks along the walkway for $20. Buyers' names were engraved or carved into the wood. Some buyers bought sections as memorial tributes for deceased relatives.

The new footpath over the bridge was officially opened on Canada Day, 1992, and some 200 people joined the inaugural walk across it and down the length of railroad track that leads to Tiger Dunlop's Tomb. The trail, still in the development stage, currently ends at the tomb. There are many obstacles still to be overcome, but some day, given the same tenacity that got them this far, the Menesetung Bridge Association will secure the trail as far as Blyth, to provide a 30-km linear walk. A more immediate goal is to raise the funding to buy Distillery Flats, just north of the bridge, for a loop trail.

Beginning at the picturesque old red brick railroad station, the trail follows the first leg of the 132-km railroad built in 1905 to join the cities of Guelph and Goderich. These cities were the first to be laid out in the more than 400,000 hectares of wilderness known as the Huron Tract. The Tract was purchased by the Canada Company in the 1820s for resale to immigrants. Land for the two cities was surveyed by Tiger Dunlop, who also pushed a road through the bush from Guelph to Goderich, so it is fitting that the trail should bear his name.

Leaving the station, the trail heads east away from the harbour, passing underneath the Harbour Street bridge. It then enters property owned by Goderich Elevators Ltd., which has granted permission for access by trail users. Huge grain elevators loom beside this section of the trail, and sometimes, massive grain-bearing ships are moored alongside. The harbour is dotted with fishing boats. A riot of wildflowers on the railroad bank to the south show how hard nature works to cover up human indiscretions, but watch out for patches of poison ivy. The trail goes down a steep embankment to North Harbour Street and crosses a set of working railroad tracks and then the highway. Be careful crossing this busy road. On the opposite side the trail goes in an easterly direction parallel to the highway about 50 m to the access

to the Menesetung Bridge. There is parking for a handful of cars here if you prefer to omit the first section of the trail.

Menesetung is the Chippewa name for the Maitland River, which is loosely interpreted to mean "where the river meets the big water" and "laughing water." The river flows wide and swift under the bridge not far from where it empties into Lake Huron. The bridge is impressive with seven concrete abutments supporting its 65-m length, high above the river. A flock of Canada geese takes off from the river and soars underneath the bridge, flying between the abutments. The view towards the city is stunning. The wide river with its islands lies in a deep, green valley with the city high on its banks. The river offers opportunities for viewing such water dwellers as muskrat, huge snapping turtles and beaver as well as a variety of ducks and geese.

The bridge was constructed in 1906, allowing extension of the rail line to the harbour. During construction a tragedy occurred when a gust of wind caught a girder, knocking three workers into the river, killing one of them instantly.

When you reach the far side of the bridge, a sign shows the Maitland Trail going off to the left, while the Tiger Dunlop Trail continues straight on. The walk down this little stretch of the Maitland Trail, known as the Mill Road Trail, makes a nice diversion. It travels through a stretch of forest that contains some Carolinian species which are at the far northern tip of their range. The most interesting of these is a massive red oak tree known as "The General." This is a heritage tree, believed to be more than 200 years old, and probably the oldest and most northerly of the Carolinian oaks located on public lands.

The trail descends into the river valley then climbs steeply out of it again. The path is bordered by lovely hardwoods and lots of vines and ferns. May-apple spreads its huge leaves across the forest floor and there are patches of poison ivy. A flock of cedar waxwings flits among the branches of a black cherry tree. The trail winds through the forest for about 1 km before reaching a lane that leads to the river bank. You will need to retrace your steps to get back to the Tiger Dunlop Trail.

Back on the Tiger Dunlop, the trail is an easy walk along a wide path between hardwood trees and shrubs, which are favoured by a flock of tiny American goldfinch. The wildflowers must be seen to be believed. We count aster, chicory, Queen Anne's lace, black-eyed Susans, milkweed, goldenrod, purple dead nettle, and beds of the gorgeous blue-fringed gentian. A mountain ash positively glows with brilliant scarlet berries and now and again, through the trees, we can catch glimpses of the Maitland River.

The track takes a wide sweep around a turn in the river and passes a gate on the left of the trail. About 50 m past here a white blaze shows the Maitland Trail going off to the right and following a set of stairs down into the valley. Just around the corner from here is a sign showing the way to Tiger Dunlop's Tomb. The path leads up to a high grassy ridge that looks out over the Maitland River, the harbour, and the city that was founded by this remarkable man. The tomb bears a plaque honouring Dr. William (Tiger) Dunlop, physician, author, woodsman, soldier, politician, and raconteur who died in 1848. His brother, Robert Graham Dunlop, who died in 1841, lies beside him.

The Tiger Dunlop Trail ends a few metres farther on when it reaches Highway 21 and stops. The original railroad bridge that crossed the highway has been removed, presenting the next challenge for the people who brought you the Menesetung Bridge.

From here, retrace your steps back along the trail and over the bridge to the parking area at the old railroad station.

Lake Superior

REGIONAL OVERVIEW

THIS AREA of rugged grandeur is the magical, mystical destination of those who want to experience Ontario's magnificent wilderness at its best. This largest of the Great Lakes has many moods, not all of them kind to humans, but that is hard to believe when the sun shines on this great expanse of blue, with its plunging cliffs, dark green hilly islands and soft sand beaches.

Hiking opportunities have blossomed over the past few years to meet a growing demand. The Trans-Canada Highway, which traverses most of Ontario's share of Lake Superior, was completed in the 1950s, and the area has always been popular with campers, anglers and hunters. Now residents and visitors want opportunities to experience the rewards of hiking into secret places that were once not easily accessible to them, and these opportunities are provided by local volunteers and provincial parks.

The major long-distance trail is the **Voyageur;** developed and maintained by local clubs with the eventual aim of joining local sections to form a 1,100 km continuous trail stretching from Manitoulin Island to Thunder Bay. It encompasses most of Ontario's Lake Superior shoreline, as well as the north shore of Lake Huron. Some 600 km have been developed to date. The Voyageur is a wilderness trail and those using it are cautioned to follow trail signs to avoid running into difficulties. Several sections have been completed on Superior's north shore. The 52.4 km **Casque Isles Section** between Terrace Bay and Rossport includes some challenging hikes, such as the six-hour climb between Schreiber and Mount Gwynne, with spectacular views of Lake Superior stretching some 80 km. Another is the hike between

Terrace Bay and Worthington Bay that hikers have named the Death Valley Section. It is one of the most remote hikes on the north shore. Portions of the trail are accessible from **Rainbow Falls Provincial Park.**

Most provincial parks on the Superior route maintain hiking trails and many do double duty as part of the Voyageur trail. **Pukaskwa National Park,** near Marathon, welcomes hikers to its portion of the Voyageur with a demanding 60 km wilderness hike on its **Coastal Hiking Trail.** Backcountry hikers must register in and out with park staff and trips must be booked in advance. There are no other access points to allow hikers to shorten this trip. Nearby **Neys Provincial Park,** located on the shoreline of Lake Superior, has short hiking trails that offer opportunities to experience the grandeur of the Lake Superior shoreline without a lot of effort. Noteworthy is the **Dune Trail** that allows exploration of unique dune vegetation. There is also the short **Point Trail,** which gives hikers a historical look at this area that housed a prisoner-of-war camp in World War II.

A major portion of the Voyageur runs through the magnificent **Lake Superior Provincial Park,** north of Sault Ste. Marie. This section is also called the **Coastal Trail,** a 63 km linear, very demanding, trail that will take up to seven days to complete, although access points allow shorter two- or three-day hikes.

There are 10 other trails in the park, including **Orphan Lake,** the **Agawa Rock Pictographs Trail,** a short but occasionally hazardous trail depending on the weather, for viewing Ojibwa rock paintings, and the two-day **Towab Trail** that takes the hiker inland to the famed Agawa Canyon.

There are stretches of the Voyageur in the **Wawa** area, just north of Lake Superior Provincial Park, including the **Bridget Lake Trail** that is rated difficult because of its remoteness. It is recommended that the trail be done in the fall. The **Magpie Trail** offers a day hike starting from the statue of the Wawa Goose, continuing along the Magpie River to Scenic High Falls (about 6 km), with the option of a further 3 km hike to Silver Falls.

Sleeping Giant Provincial Park, on the Sibley Peninsula near Thunder Bay, offers a variety of trails ranging from easy to strenuous that are some of the best in this area. The highlight is **The Chest,** a

16 km trail that leads to a view over the head of The Giant, the mountain that appears in profile as a giant at rest. Ojibwa culture says the figure is that of Nanabijou, a revered teacher. Other trails in this lovely park lead the hiker through stands of old-growth white pine and to view unusual plants. Moose are often seen around some of the inland lakes.

The City of Thunder Bay Parks and Recreation offers short trails around the city, as does Lakehead Region Conservation.

Bay Points Trail, Casque Isles Sections, Voyageur Trail

Terrace Bay

• **LENGTH:** 8 km (4 hours) • **DEGREE OF DIFFICULTY:** Moderate
• **TYPE OF TRAIL:** Linear • **LOCATION:** Terrace Bay

HOW TO GET THERE:

Access to both ends of the Bay Points Trail is close to Highway 17, the Trans-Canada Highway, just west of the town of Terrace Bay. This trail description covers the walk from east to west. It is recommended that you park a vehicle at the western end of the trail and have someone drive you back to the eastern approach, so that

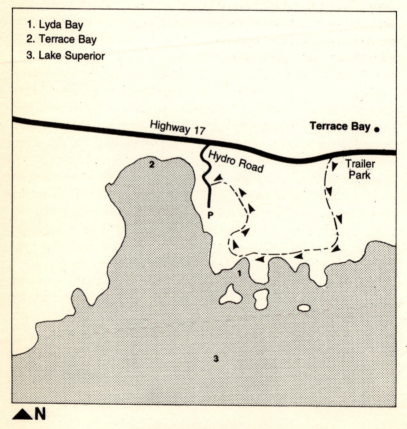

1. Lyda Bay
2. Terrace Bay
3. Lake Superior

you can start the trail there and hike back to your vehicle parked at the western end, which is on Hydro Road, just west of Terrace Bay off Highway 17.

The trail start is about .5 km south of Highway 17, from a parking lot at the Aguasabon Gorge, some 2.5 km east of Hydro Road on Highway 17. Look for the Aguasabon Gorge signs close to a campground on the western outskirts of town. A short drive leads to the parking lot where the trail begins. There is no charge for using the trail, but donations to the Voyageur Trail Club are welcome. Volunteers have done an excellent job placing trail markers, and if you follow them there is little chance of getting lost. However, the trail is not well travelled, so it is advisable to tell someone where you intend to hike and your expected return time.

• • •

This is a gorgeous trail that traverses the lonely shoreline of Lake Superior, visiting pristine beaches where the only tracks in the sand are those of moose and black bear. There are stunning views of this magnificent and mysterious lake, with glimpses at the equally mysterious Slate Islands, which are home to a herd of woodland caribou. You'll travel over ancient boulder beaches, encrusted with lichens, that were shorelines of a much larger prehistoric lake, and there are many opportunities for wildlife viewing. The area also has arguably the best blueberry patch anywhere—for just about the entire length of the trail.

Before starting the trail, which leads sharply downhill on a wide path from the parking lot, take a look at the gorge and waterfalls of the Aguasabon River from viewing platforms in the parking lot. It's awesome. The trail itself mirrors the abrupt 30 m drop of the Aguasabon by descending steeply from the start—one good reason for beginning the hike here, instead of encountering the steepness at the end if you did the trail from west to east. The town of Terrace Bay is so named because it is built on high terraces left by receding glaciers, which explains the sharp drop for the hiker to get to the lakeshore. Just minutes from the parking lot we come across bear droppings on the wide path, which appears to have once been used as a road. The walking is good here, and it continues for about 25 minutes, almost to the lakeshore, when the trail turns abruptly to the right, enters the forest, and becomes a narrow path.

The path continues through the forest, close to the beach. The blueberry bushes are laden and tracks show that a moose has walked the trail a little earlier in the day. Soon you emerge onto an attractive sandy beach and the trail winds around a small bay. This is a great spot for lunch, but keep going because there are equally good places, if not better. From the beach, the trail continues through the forest until it emerges again onto a small boulder beach, which offers some challenging walking. Back into the forest, with more moose tracks and more blueberry bushes, the trail goes over another boulder beach, goes back into the forest, and then comes out onto a delightful sandy beach where the Slate Islands are visible in the distance to the west.

From this point the trail goes inland and climbs into a rocky area, then reaches the gorgeous sandy beach of Lyda Bay, the highlight of the trip. Walk around the beach to the right, jump a stream, and there are old logs and rocks that invite the hiker to take off the pack and eat lunch. We munch, hoping that the moose that left the tracks in the sand will return for a photo opportunity. Just up from the beach are the remains of an old log cabin—a reminder that the fur traders of yesterday earned their living in this area. It is not hard to imagine even earlier fur traders—the voyageurs of the Northwest Company—travelling by canoe between Old Fort William at the western end of Lake Superior and Montreal, pausing to rest in this safe haven, as well as early explorers and missionaries.

Continuing through the forest the trail reaches an ancient raised boulder beach and, again, there is some pretty tough walking to cross it. Take the time to examine some of the unusual lichens—some of them look like colourful cacti. After re-entering the forest, the trail starts to meander uphill until it reaches a high rocky ridge, which you must climb. From the top of this ridge there are great views of the lake and some of the beaches. The trail winds around the cliff edge and then you must descend by way of a wooden ladder. From here the trail crosses another raised boulder beach, goes back into the woods, and continues on to the final, but most challenging, ancient boulder beach. A cairn with a trail marker sits in the middle pointing the way to the left, through the woods and underneath a cliff. Just after you reach a sign that reads "Hydro Bay" you will negotiate a small stream, cross a dry land area thick with sphagnum moss, and then enter a brushy area. Climb a couple more ridges and you come to the top of one that offers a fine view of the bay known as Terrace Bay, and the hydro tower that is your destination. From here the trail continues through the forest, over another ridge and onto a wide path that leads quickly to Hydro Road. From here it is a short walk downhill to your vehicle.

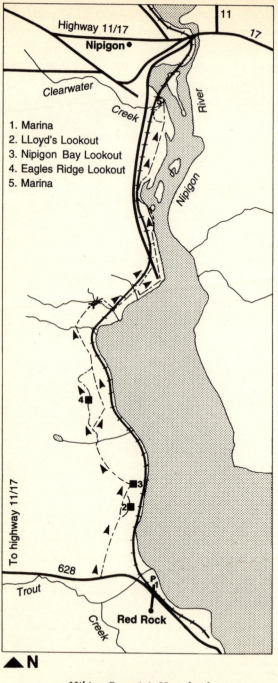

1. Marina
2. LLoyd's Lookout
3. Nipigon Bay Lookout
4. Eagles Ridge Lookout
5. Marina

Highway 11/17

Nipigon

Clearwater

Creek

Nipigon

River

11

17

To highway 11/17

628

Trout

Creek

Red Rock

N

Red Rock to Nipigon Trail

Nipigon, Lake Superior

- **LENGTH:** 9 km (4 to 5 hours)
- **DEGREE OF DIFFICULTY:** Moderate • **TYPE OF TRAIL:** Linear
- **LOCATION:** Nipigon, North Shore of Lake Superior

HOW TO GET THERE:

The town of Red Rock lies approximately 110 km northeast of Thunder Bay. Nipigon is some 10 km farther north at the northernmost reach of Lake Superior. Both towns are accessible from Highway 11/17, the Trans-Canada Highway. From the Trans-Canada, take Highway 628 to the town of Red Rock and look for the Vicmor Hotel. The trail starts on the east side of the highway, close to the hotel. There is a small parking lot, or you can park at the marina on the lakefront and walk back to the trail entrance. This is not a loop trail, so car jockeying is necessary. If you are a visitor to the area and car jockeying is difficult, there is a taxi service in Nipigon. There is no charge for using this trail, which is maintained by volunteers; however, donations are welcome. The Red Rock to Nipigon trail over Paju Mountain is a completed section of the unfinished 21 km Nipigon River Trail, which will follow the route of this renowned Ontario river. It also forms a section of the Voyageur Trail, a series of local trails that stretch between Manitoulin Island and Thunder Bay.

• • •

The trail is rated moderate because of its length, but be prepared for some adventures. If you take the loop trails off the main trail— and you should—you will be rewarded with magnificent views, but will be descending fairly steep inclines, with the help of strategically placed ropes. There is also some rockhopping to be done as well as a little rock climbing. The trail is well marked in most areas and the path is well trodden. There is no danger of getting lost, but do tell someone where you are going. Hiking boots are essential. The trail winds through the boreal forest with side trails leading to lookouts over Lake Superior, the town of Red Rock with its pulp mill, and the Nipigon River where it flows into Nipigon Bay. The major attraction is the lookout from Eagle Ridge, which offers a prime viewing site. The small town of Nipigon appears as a toy village and the view spreads north to the famous Palisades, noted for their popularity with ice climbers, then eastwards to the Kama Hill. There are magnificent vistas of Lake Superior and the islands of Nipigon Bay.

The trail from Red Rock starts over a good, wide trail covered with the chipped red stone the area is named for. The route travels through a thick forest of evergreens, mountain maple and poplar. Benches fashioned from whatever is available are placed strategically on the long upward trek that starts immediately from the parking lot. There are also bird feeders and interpretive stations. This meticulously groomed section of trail lasts only until the first lookout, indicating that this stretch is a popular walk for locals. A similar stretch is close to the town of Nipigon and again, it is a popular local walk.

The first lookout requires a diversion from the main trail but it is well marked. Called Lloyd's Lookout, after the resident who developed this section of the trail, it overlooks the Lake Superior shoreline to the south, west and east, showing the numerous islands in Nipigon Bay that are about to become part of a new national marine park. The pulp mill is plainly visible. A plaque, donated by the mill, directs the hiker's attention eastwards to Kama Bay, in the far distance, from where Van Horne's troops marched across the ice to Red Rock during the Riel Rebellion in the 1880s, because that section of the railroad had not yet been completed. The Nipigon Bay area was the last completed section of the CPR, in 1885, because difficult terrain made this particular stretch very expensive to develop.

The continuation of the trail from Lloyd's Lookout is somewhat confusing and is not well marked, but there is no danger of getting lost. You can either retrace your steps to the main trail, or turn eastwards and look for an unmarked path. You'll have to do some rock climbing, using the rope that volunteers have placed there, to the next lookout, which offers a similar vista but from a higher point. From here the path drops down about 200 m to rejoin the main trail.

The path now becomes a narrow trail twisting through the forest and over a couple of log bridges and through some boggy areas, with occasional glimpses of the coastline. Underfoot, the soils are thin and coral lichen and Labrador tea cling to the rocks. At this altitude, the deciduous trees have given way to jack pines and black spruce. The trail continues high above the river, and you can see through the trees the steep hills of its far shore and the mountainous islands in Lake Superior's Nipigon Bay. In the soft mud of the trail we come upon fresh moose tracks.

Where there is a signpost pointing the way back to Red Rock, the trail becomes a steep, wide slope and at the bottom turns sharply to the left where there is a sign pointing to Nipigon. Continue downhill to a marshy area, cross it, and you will come to a ridge where there is a rope to help you haul yourself up. The trail continues over the ridge and down the other side to cross a stream by means of stepping-stones, then climbs steeply again. At the top of this neverending hill there is a sign pointing to Eagle Ridge and this trail goes off to the left uphill. You have a choice here of taking the Eagle Ridge side trail or continuing on the main trail which gives you another opportunity to visit this outstanding lookout farther along.

The main trail now joins a hydro corridor and swings downhill to the right. From an open area you can see the Nipigon River and Doghead Mountain on its eastern bank. From here the trail becomes extremely challenging, with some rock climbing and rock-hopping along the increasingly narrow path. Quite unexpectedly you emerge onto Eagle Ridge and all the rigors of the trail are forgotten as you savour the breathtaking views from this 300 m-high cliff top. There is the river mouth and the town in the distance, to the north forested hills roll to infinity, and in Lake Superior the primeval looking islands thrust skywards.

Unfortunately, when you are up this high you must also descend, and shortly after leaving the ridge the path leads quickly and steeply down from the cliff. Sturdy ropes make a handy guardrail. Continuing downwards, with a bit more rock scrambling here and there, the trail reaches swampy ground, passes through some woods, and crosses the Stillwater Creek. The trail crosses two sets of railroad tracks, and the hiker soon has a choice of taking a shortcut to Nipigon along a paved road or continuing the trail down to the lakeshore to the site of an old pulp mill and following the river bank to the Nipigon marina where the trail ends.

Orphan Lake Loop

Lake Superior Provincial Park, Wawa

- **LENGTH:** 8 km (3 to 4 hours)
- **DEGREE OF DIFFICULTY:** Moderate • **TYPE OF TRAIL:** Loop
  LOCATION: Lake Superior Provincial Park, Wawa

HOW TO GET THERE:

Lake Superior Provincial Park is located on Highway 17, the Trans-Canada Highway, between Sault Ste. Marie and Wawa. The trail is close to the centre of the park, south of Gargantua Road and north of Katherine Cove on the west side. There is a good highway sign indicating its location. There is parking for a dozen

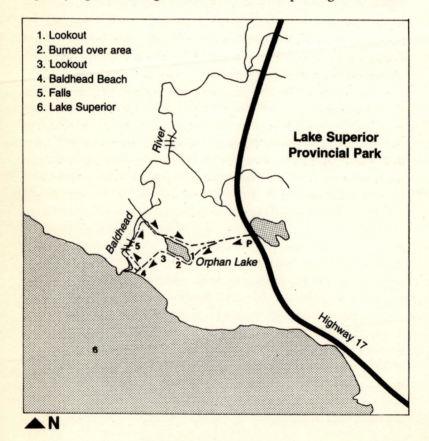

1. Lookout
2. Burned over area
3. Lookout
4. Baldhead Beach
5. Falls
6. Lake Superior

Lake Superior Provincial Park

River

Baldhead

Orphan Lake

Highway 17

▲ N

or so vehicles and the trail starts right from the parking lot. There are pit toilets at the start of the trail. At the parking lot you must purchase a day-use pass from the self-serve stand and display the pass on your vehicle's dashboard.

• • •

While the Orphan Lake Trail is far from being the longest or most challenging trail in this spectacular provincial park, it is probably the most diverse, giving the hiker a microcosmic taste of what the park has to offer. It includes a visit to a pretty little interior lake, an isolated Lake Superior beach, waterfalls, and a view of magnificent Lake Superior that the non-hiking visitor to the park never sees. The park is one of the jewels of the provincial park system, with almost 115 km of Lake Superior coastline. The shoreline was designated Ontario's Heritage Coast by the provincial government in recognition of its unique qualities. The Orphan Lake Trail is rated moderate because it is fairly short, but it is rugged due to the numerous rocky climbs and extremely slippery surfaces. Hiking boots are a must. Don't do this trail in running shoes.

At the point where the trail emerges onto the Lake Superior shoreline it joins up with the 63 km Coastal Trail, which, as the name implies, traverses the Lake Superior shoreline through the park from Agawa Bay to Chalfant Cove. The Orphan Lake Trail is well blazed, and hikers should note that whenever a sign indicates a side trail off from the main trail it should be taken, since these are to the lookouts that the trail is famous for. If you stick to the main trail you will miss them. All side trails are very short.

From the parking lot the trail winds through a forest of sugar maple and yellow birch, and the forest floor is alive with the white flowers and brilliant red berries of the bunchberry, setting off the dark green of ferns and multicoloured fungi. Sugar maples are at the northernmost reach of their range here and their vivid reds are outstanding in the fall. Common birdlife includes the northern three-toed woodpecker, the hairy woodpecker, the kinglet, and a variety of spring and fall warblers.

About 30 m along the trail, with the noise of the highway fading, you will come to a small log bridge that is quite slippery, and then the trail meanders uphill in a northerly direction. Almost immediately you will start a long, twisting climb, which will culminate in a fork in the trail. This is where the loop starts. The trail sign here suggests following the path leading to the left, so that's the one we took. Some 30 m further along there is a sign indicating a side trail, and this leads quickly to the first lookout. Here you will stand on a cliff overlooking tiny Orphan Lake. Get your camera out. A sign tells us that the lake was named by a family from Agawa Bay that trapped in the area between the 1930s and 1970s. One winter night, after snowshoeing into the then un-named lake two family members were unable to make it back to camp and they stayed at the lake. One of the family remarked that they looked like two lonely orphans, and the name stuck.

From the lookout, the main trail goes down a steep incline and levels out to cross a boardwalk, continuing downhill and into a brushy area where there are slippery rocks. The descent leads you to the shoreline of Orphan Lake and you can glimpse it as you walk past. The trail skirts the lake about halfway and leads into an area where there was a forest fire in 1998. The blackened trees are still standing and you can see new growth. Climbing away from the lake you will encounter another side trail, which involves a short, very steep climb to a lookout over Lake Superior's Baldhead Beach, the halfway point of the hike. The views are breathtaking, especially on a sunny day when the lake reflects the stunning blue of sunny skies.

From here, the main trail winds sharply downhill, and you will be doing lots of rockhopping. Take a quick look at the rocks and note the bands of quartz running through them. Shortly, when you emerge onto the beach, you will need to resist stuffing your back-pack with the gorgeous pebbles that have been washed smooth by eons of Lake Superior wave action and ice friction. Like all park property, the stones are protected.

The beach offers an ideal spot for lunch and an excuse to spend a little time in this special place. An especially good site is at the northerly end, where the Baldhead River enters the lake and the return leg of the trail starts. Some large driftwood offers good seating. You are now on both the Orphan Lake Trail and the Coastal Trail.

Orphan Lake Trail continues by following the river inland a little way as it winds through forested hills. After a short incline you will come to a set of rapids, followed by views of some impressive waterfalls. When you reach a sturdy bridge, use it to take a look at the falls, but don't cross since this marks the division between the two trails and continuation of the Coastal Trail. Several short side trails on the Orphan Lake Trail allow views of the falls at various levels.

Leaving the falls, the trail goes downhill, then offers some easy walking for a short way through the forest until you come to another incline, then down to a boardwalk. From here the trail climbs steeply and you'll be doing more rockhopping, then the trail narrows and a ravine falls sharply away to your left. Very soon you will come to the foot of a huge granite cliff. After hiking alongside you arrive at the northern shore of Orphan Lake. The trail skirts this end of the lake and across it you can see the burned over area that you hiked through earlier. After climbing a ridge you will come to the fork in the trail that signifies the end of the loop. From here on the trail follows the main path back through the woods to the parking lot.

APPENDIX
Some Useful Addresses

HIKING ASSOCIATIONS:

Hike Ontario!
Suite 411, 1185 Eglinton Ave. East, Toronto, Ontario M3C 3C6
Tel: (416) 426-7362 Fax: (416) 426-7045
Website: http://hikeontario.com/
  Provincial umbrella group of long-distance trail associations. Provides information on trails across the province and details on member trail associations. Promotes walking, hiking and trail development in Ontario.

Rails to Trails Association
c/o Hike Ontario!

Avon Trail Association
P.O. Box 21148, Stratford, Ontario N5A 7V4
Website: http://home.golden.net/~wlindsch/avon/avon.htm

Bruce Trail Association
P.O. Box 857, Hamilton, Ontario L8N 3N9
Tel: (905) 529-6821 (24-hour answering machine)
Toll free: 1-800-665-HIKE Fax: (905) 529-6823
Website: http://brucetrail.org

Elgin Hiking Trail Club
Box 250, St. Thomas, Ontario N5P 3T9

Ganaraska Trail Association
P.O. Box 693, Orillia, Ontario L3V 6K7
Website: http://www3.sympatico.ca/hikers.net/ganarask.htm

Grand Valley Trails Association
Box 1233, Kitchener, Ontario N2G 4G8

Guelph Trail Club
Box 1, Guelph, Ontario N1H 6J6

Maitland Trail Association
P.O. Box 433, Goderich, Ontario N7A 4C7

Oak Ridges Trail Association
P.O. Box 28544, Aurora, Ontario L4G 6S6
Website: http://www.interlog.com/~orta

Rideau Trail Association
Box 15, Kingston, Ontario K7L 4V6
Website: http://www.ncf.carleton.ca/RTA

Thames Valley Trail Association
Box 821, Terminal "B", London, Ontario N6A 4Z3

Thunder Bay Hiking Club
P.O. Box 10041, Thunder Bay, Ontario P7B 6T6
Website: http://www.tbha.baynet.net/

Voyageur Trail Association
Box 66, Sault Ste. Marie, Ontario P6A 5L2
Toll free: 1-800-393-5353, then select message #9999
Website: http://www3.sympatico.ca/voyageur.trail

OTHER SOURCES OF INFORMATION:

Ministry of Natural Resources
Public Information Centre, Queen's Park, Toronto, Ontario M7A 1W3
Tel: (416) 314-2000 Fax: (416) 314-1593 Toll free: 1-800-667-1940
Website: http://www.mnr.gov.on.ca
  (topographic maps; information on provincial parks, Conservation Authorities and Crown Lands; district office telephone numbers)

Ontario Travel
Queen's Park, Toronto, Ontario M7A 2E5
Tel: (416) 314-0944 Toronto and area
Toll free: 1-800-268-3736 Fax: (416) 314-7372
Telecommunication Device for the Deaf - T.D.D.
Tel: (416) 314-6557 (or call collect)
Website: http://www.ontario-canada.com
  (Information about Ontario outfitters offering packaged hiking vacations; information about regional tourist facilities and accommodations)

Ontario Ministry of Transportation
1201 Wilson Avenue, Downsview, Ontario M3M 1J8
Tel: (416) 235-4339 Toll free: 1-800-268-4686
Website: http://www.mto.gov.on.ca
  (Ontario Transportation Map Series, scale 1:250,000. Detailed maps of regions across the province show sideroads and county roads, as well as major highways)

THE HIKER'S CODE

- *Hike only on marked routes—do not leave the trail, especially when walking on private land.*

- *Use stiles, and close gates behind you. Do not climb fences.*

- *Leave the trail cleaner than you found it. Pack everything out that you packed in.*

- *Do not pick wildflowers and plants, trample on seedlings, damage live trees or strip off bark. Our planet is a fragile one.*

- *Keep dogs on a leash.*

- *Protect and do not disturb wildlife.*

- *Light fires only in campsite fireplaces. Carry a lightweight stove.*

- *Camp only in designated campsites.*

- *Respect the privacy of nearby landowners by parking responsibly, quietly, and without blocking lanes or driveways.*

- *Leave only your thanks. Take nothing but photographs.*

Index

About the Author and the Illustrator

Shirley Dallison Teasdale
(photo by Heather Bickle)

SHIRLEY TEASDALE is an avid walker and hiker, whose love of the sport began in her native Lake District in northern England. Her childhood friendship with Beatrix Potter was an early influence on her decision to become a writer about natural subjects. She has written extensively about Ontario's outdoors, including weekly contributions to *The Globe and Mail* from 1976 to 1982. Since 1982 she has been employed in various communications capacities by the Ontario government. She lives with her husband, Ken, and a fat orange cat in Bramalea, Ontario.

SHAYNA LABELLE-BEADMAN is an artist who has had an interest in the outdoors since her childhood in Cochrane, Ontario. She has won a number of awards for wildlife sketches, and annually donates work to Ducks Unlimited for fundraising. She is a publications and exhibits specialist with the Ontario Government.